BOB RYDER ON COACHING COLLEGIATE ARCHERY

BOB RYDER ON COACHING COLLEGIATE ARCHERY

Part of the Watching Arrows Fly
Coaching Library

Library of Congress Cataloging-in Publication Data

Bob Ryder on Coaching Collegiate Archery / Bob Ryder.
  p. cm
  ISBN 978-0-578-58651-9 (softcover)
  1. Archery. 2. Coaching Bob Ryder, 1951-

ISBN: 978-0-578-58651-9

The web addresses cited in this text were current as of August 2019, unless otherwise noted.

Writer: Bob Ryder; Copy Editor: Steve Ruis; Proofreader: Steve Ruis; Cover Designer: Steve Ruis; Layout: Steve Ruis; Photographers (cover and interior): Bob Ryder unless noted otherwise; Illustrators: Steve Ruis and Bob Ryder

Printed in the United States of America 10 9 8 7 6 5 4 3 2 1

Watching Arrows Fly
www.watchingarrowsfly.com

Dedication

I dedicate this book to Rob and Lynnette Wheatcroft who allowed their son, Adam Wheatcroft, to come all the way from Michigan to James Madison University in Harrisonburg, Virginia to shoot for us. Adam was a great kid and a great archer who won National and World Titles for us at JMU but lost his battle with brain cancer as a senior. The Wheatcrofts told me that JMU Archery was the most important thing in Adam's life his last three years and they set up the Adam Wheatcroft Memorial Fund to support it, working tirelessly to help fund the team ever since. The JMU Archery Team owes much of its success to the generosity and love the Wheatcrofts have shared over the years.

Adam Wheatcroft in 1998.

I also dedicate this book to my wife, Deb Ryder, who has supported me in my lifetime affair with the Sport of Archery . . . at least to the point of taking the deadbolt off to allow me back into the house after my many archery trips.

Bob Ryder
August 2019

Contents

Never did I imagine I would receive the awards I have. Here I am receiving the Maurice Thompson Award from the CEO of USA Archery. All awards aside, coaching a college archery team is very rewarding in and of itself.

Preface

A few years ago, Steve Ruis asked me to write an article on coaching archery from the perspective of a college archery coach. After giving it some thought I agreed to write an article to help other coaches to start or grow their archery teams based on my 20+ years of experience as Head Archery Coach of one of the most successful archery programs in the country, that of James Madison University.

One article turned into thirty or so and we thought it might be time to put together a book aimed at helping all collegiate archery coaches. Any coach working with a college team, a JOAD Club, or any other group of archers will benefit from the information included in this book.

Several of the chapters in this book are written on topics that have not been addressed in other books due to the team or group twist that this perspective provides. And you will find a considerable amount of the book deals with the mental game of archery in an effort to address the tools you need to develop your team's mental game as well as a chapter on how to put it all together. I have also included a significant amount of information on equipment from helping your new archers select their equipment to setting it up as well as tuning it to maximize their performance.

If you are interested in coaching archery, whether it's for a college or a JOAD, 4-H or other club, you will be required to become certified. I think it's great if you follow "The BEST Method" to a tee or if you are old school and still teach the "9 Steps to the 10 Ring." Both methods have produced Olympic medals for us here in the United States.

The nice thing about archery is that there is not just one way to do anything and if you are doing something that is wrong in someone else's mind . . . as long as you do it exactly the same every time . . . you win!

1

Bob Ryder

Getting Started

This photo was taken upon the night of our return from competing in the US Intercollegiate Archery Championship in Sparta, IL. The success of this team was unprecedented. Their accomplishments are listed below.

2007 National Champion – Men's Compound: Braden Gellenthien
2007 National Champion – Women's Compound: Brittany Lorenti
2007 National Champion – Men's Recurve: Nate McCullough
2007 National Champion – Men's Compound Team:
Braden Gellenthien, Jedd Greshock, Michael Ashton, Steve Schwade
2007 National Champion – Women's Compound Team:
Brittany Lorenti, Jessica Fasula, Raleigh Maupin, Kimberly Dobbins
2007 National Champion – Mixed Compound Team:
Braden Gellenthien, Brittany Lorenti, Jedd Greshock, Jessica Fasula
2007 National Champion – Men's Recurve Team:
Nate McCullough, Jacob Wukie, Curt Briscoe, David Lipsey, Nick Kale
2007 National Champion – Mixed Recurve Team:
Nate McCullough, Katie Jepson, Jacob Wukie, Amy McAleese
2007 National Champion – Overall Team:
Compound Men (Braden Gellenthien, Jedd Greshock, Michael Ashton,
Steve Schwade); Compound Women (Brittany Lorenti, Jessica Fasula,
Raleigh Maupin, Kimberly Dobbins); Recurve Men (Nate McCullough,
Jacob Wukie, Curt Briscoe, David Lipsey, Nick Kale); Recurve Women
(Katie Jepson, Amy McAleese, Katy Bienvenu, Geetha Mathew)
2007 National Coach of the Year – Bob Ryder
Assistant Coaches (Andy Puckett and Megan Bowker)

1

Taking the Leap into Coaching Collegiate Archery

Every person who becomes involved with coaching archery has their own unique story as to how it all began. The fun thing about college archery teams is that no matter how you get started, you can make as much of an impact in collegiate archery as you choose.

Some of us were fortunate to have applied for, interviewed for, and been hired for an archery coaching position, but these opportunities seem to be quite rare. It really doesn't matter if you are a paid full-time coach, a part-timer, an unpaid volunteer, or simply the father of an archer who has just enrolled in college, you can choose to create a team that competes with even the best teams in the country. One of the best things about U.S.A. Archery's Collegiate Archery Program (CAP) is that the most important purpose of that association is to provide the opportunity to every full-time college student in the U.S. to compete. We work just as hard to provide opportunities to a one-person team in Montana as we provide to a 20-person team in Pennsylvania.

Archery is an individual sport that has successfully turned itself into a team sport in collegiate competition. So, I encourage you to look at your role as a coach in an individual sport, take a leap of faith, and be the agent at your institution who allows the development of a full team and helps to grow the sport we love. Let me explain.

What coaches outside the world of collegiate archery are used to is teaching and coaching individual archers to compete in individual competitions, each in pursuit of a single title in their division. What makes coaching archery in college such a blast is that while each of the archers on your team is competing for individual titles in single elimination Olympic Rounds (OR) in their respective divisions, they are also often competing in single elimination three-person team competitions in each of the same categories (including Men's Recurve, Women's Recurve, Men's Compound and Women's Compound,

Men's Bowhunter, Women's Bowhunter, Men's Barebow, and Women's Barebow) and single elimination mixed team competitions in Recurve, Compound, Bowhunter, and Barebow (one male and one female). If that is not enough to build interest in team competition, the results of all of these team competitions are compiled along with individual results to determine an Overall Team Champion. These are the categories for CAP competition. As more groups get involved, 3-D, field archery, etc. other opportunities will become available.

If you haven't noticed, I'm talking about taking you out of your coaching comfort zone, tearing that page out of your playbook and setting it on fire. Time's up! If you are crazy enough to still be reading this then I assume you are open-minded enough to take a new look at your role as a coach. I am suggesting that if you take this leap, your coaching will no longer be about you building your resume by simply coaching the best talent in your area or coaching individuals who are so motivated they re-energize you. You will be entering a world where you encourage non-archers to become archers, bowhunters to become target archers, recreational archers to become competitive archers and, in the end, develop a group of individuals with varying degrees of commitment into a real team.

There are few experiences in life that can be more challenging than this and even fewer that you will find to be more rewarding than taking this journey. And in the process, you will find that you have helped to turn the boys and girls you've worked with into young men and women who you are proud to call your friends.

Finding Your Team

It's time to talk about how you find your team. If you are already coaching an individual at a local college, you already have your starting point. If not, you can contact the Collegiate Archery Program at collegiate@usarchery.org for a list of schools in your area who have at least one registered collegiate archer and simply make your services available.

I was excited to meet my team when I was hired to coach at James Madison University (JMU). To my dismay, I had inherited eight recurve archers including seven men and only one woman. Not only did I not have a women's recurve team (three archers are required), I didn't even have a mixed recurve team (at the time, 1992, two men and two women were required). I suffered through my first season with my men's team placing in all our competitions but with our whole team barely making the radar screen. It was at that time that I decided I had more control over my own team's fate.

I started encouraging young archers to choose JMU for their education and when classes started in the fall, I put posters up on campus inviting students (especially women) to come to an open house to meet the archery team and discuss opportunities to join the team. At the same time, I asked the team members to go out on campus, find women that they would like to have on the team and, if necessary, drag them to the meeting (metaphorically, of course). When we had the open house, the guys had brought enough gals that the success of our recruitment was then up to me. I explained to them that my vision for JMU Archery was to develop a team that could compete with any-one in the country, would produce All-Americans and would strive to win a National Championship, and if they were willing to work hard and were open to change, that they could be a part of something great. Twenty years, and 42 All-Americans, and 16 National Champions, and 23 National Team Titles and 14 World Champions later (as of 2019). . . I believe I held up my end of that bargain.

That first year we had fewer than ten kids from campus come to that open house. Since then we have learned a few more tricks. Last year we set up a booth at Student Organization Night and ended up with 150 kids signing up for archery and most of them shot with the club throughout the first semester until we started cutting to make things manageable.

Immediate Needs

If you have an immediate need for team members:

1. **Plan an Open House**
   Find a time and date for an Archery Team Open House and Demonstration to be held at the location used for team practices. If none has been established use a local pro-shop or archery club.

2. **Archery Classes**
   Some colleges still offer archery classes for credit. If that is the case at your school, you have a gold mine. Simply visit the classes toward the middle or end of the course to recruit more interested and possibly tal-ented students for your team. However, before you make this visit, be sure to clear it with the instructor of the class so they aren't surprised or put-off by the reason for your visit.

3. **On-Campus**
   Put up flyers at strategic locations around campus advertising the open house and the team (get permission to post them first). Obviously, this is your source for kids with little to no background in competitive archery.

4. **Local Pro Shops**
   Visit local pro shops and ask if they know of any current customers who

are attending your college, ask permission to put up a poster (or flyer) and leave them business cards for any kids who show an interest. Here we hope to find kids already interested in bowhunting.

5. **Local Archery Clubs**
   Visit all the local archery or sportsmen's clubs asking to put up posters and leaving cards at each. This is where we hope to find kids who already have an interest in target archery.

Planning for the Future

Planting the seeds for success and continuity of your program requires you to establish a presence. People need to know you are there.

1. **Set up a Archery Team Website**
   Let potential archery recruits know what is going on with your archery team. Kids looking for a place to go to school will want to know about your schedule, your success, your facilities, your roster and other info you find appropriate such as your qualifications as a coach. It is an opportunity for these kids to explore your team as well as others in an unthreatening manner.

2. **Your Visibility**
   Get more involved with tournaments on a local, state, and national level. By volunteering at or attending these events potential recruits can see how involved and committed you are, and by getting to meet and talk to you they will be more inclined to choose your school to attend. Your name can become synonymous with the team so that when they hear one name they naturally relate the other.

3. **Team Visibility**
   Team uniforms should be selected to give the team a look they can all be proud of. While it may be difficult to get publicity for your team in local newspapers and other independent media, you should be able to develop a relationship with the sports writers or reporters for campus clubs and organizations with the school paper.

4. **Be More than a Team**
   Let your team know that they have an opportunity to be more than just a team and encourage them to discuss what is really important to them and to become involved in charitable activities that make them feel good about themselves and their involvement in the community. If they do get involved they will make it easy to for you to find a way to bring attention to them while they make these contributions.

Just as the reputation you have built serves you, the reputation your team builds will serve them.

Final Remarks

I am encouraging you to build a complete team by showing you how to find your team and how to give that team a reasonable life expectancy. Of course, you will be needing equipment. While you can do fundraising and get a small budget as a club sport, I recommend you look into an equipment grant from the Easton Sports Development Foundation. They have been extremely generous in their support of collegiate archery programs. You can find more information about these opportunities and apply for a grant at www.teamusa.org/USA-Archery.

2

Collegiate Archery Competition

I must confess, I have enjoyed every archery tournament I have ever been to. It doesn't matter whether I was shooting or coaching or if it were warm and calm or blowing snow. My worst days on the shooting field have always been better than my best days doing almost anything else.

That said, collegiate competitions are the most fun. Indoor competitions to date have remained pretty much the same for all competitors' collegiate divisions simply added to the mix. The real fun comes outdoors.

The U.S. National Outdoor Collegiate Championships (USNOCC's) is seriously one of the best archery tournaments on the planet. It is designed after the Olympic Games, including a two-day 70m Qualifying Round, a single elimination FITA Olympic Round for Individual Competition, and both Team Rounds and Mixed Team Rounds. While the possibility of change exists for any event the Tournament Schedule used in 2019 is included in this chapter as an example (*see p. 15*).

Once the format of the USNOCC's is established it is up to you, as a collegiate coach, to prepare your team for the event. While you can shoot the various rounds in practice, it is much more effective to give them real tournament experience with these formats. There is such a wide range in experience and skill level in collegiate competition it is imperative that every effort be made to prepare your team, especially your younger and less experienced archers, for what and who they will be facing. In the east this can be challenging because the USNOCC's is typically in May near the end of the school year and this can be very soon after there is snow on the ground outside.

One of the ways that I have chosen to level the playing field has been to work on improving my team's comfort zone at the US Intercollegiate Championships. The first major step that I took to help all of our collegiate archers in the east to become better prepared for USNOCC's is to use an abbreviated version of the USNOCC's tournament format for all outdoor competitions in our area.

Our very first outdoor tournament of the season is the Adam Wheatcroft Memorial held on the campus of James Madison University in Harrisonburg, VA. We shoot a 70-meter Qualifying Round, Individual Elimination Matches, Team Rounds and Mixed Team Rounds. This same format is used at the New England Collegiate Archery Tournament and at the Eastern Regional Archery Championship on the campus of Penn College in Williamsport, PA.

We initially set the events up to start at noon on Saturday and end no later than 3 pm on Sunday to allow teams to travel the 5-7 hours to the event and limit their motel requirements to one night. The event has now grown so large that we are forced to start the qualifying round on Saturday morning in order to complete all the competition on one weekend. The qualifying round consists of twelve six-arrow ends all shot at 70 m. At the end of the qualifying round the scores are tallied and the archers are seeded for the individual elimination matches that will be shot the next morning.

The event continues the next morning at 8 AM when the individual elimination rounds begin. The archers find what their individual seed is in their division and then have to shoot their way to victory through a tournament bracket that works just like the one used each year and made famous by the NCAA basketball tournament. This single elimination round is shot in three-arrow ends with some variations between Recurve and Compound competitions.

Compound and Bowhunter archers shoot five three-arrow ends with the archer having the higher score winning the match. Recurve and Barebow archers win two "match points" for each three-arrow end that they win. If the archers tie an end they each win one match point. The first archer to win six match points wins the match. Matches that are tied after five ends will be decided by a one arrow shoot off (Recurve, Compound, Bowhunter, and Barebow). The one-on-one competitions continue with one archer retiring at the end of each match until four archers are left in each division. With four archers left we shoot the semi-finals. At the completion of that match the two archers losing in the semi-finals will shoot for a Bronze Medal and the two semi-final winning archers shoot for the Gold and Silver.

Next each college is given brackets and target assignments for the team rounds. Men's Recurve, Women's Recurve, Men's Compound, Women's Compound, Men's Bowhunter, Women's Bowhunter teams line up and go at it in the same single elimination format that the individual competition used. Don't be shocked when you attend or compete in your first Collegiate Team Round competition. It has a tendency to be loud and raucous with a lot of cheering, screaming, and animated fans. It's a tag team event with three archers shooting six arrows in two minutes. The event starts with all archers one meter behind the shooting line. When time begins one archer on each team goes to the line to shoot his arrows. Archer #1 shoots one (or two) arrows and leaves the shooting line. Once Archer #1 passes the one-meter line Archer #2 goes to the line and shoots one (or two) arrows and then leaves the shooting line. Once Archer #2 passes the one-meter line Archer #3 goes to the line and shoots one (or two) arrows. This continues until all three archers have shot their two arrows or until time expires. You are allowed to have a coach in a box on the shooting line for coaching and encouragement and while he can have binoculars, he can't spot for the archers. Archers must be careful to make their exchanges cleanly because if more than one archer or one archer's equipment occupies the area inside of the one-meter line it is a violation. With the first violation, the team receives a Yellow Card. Subsequent violations result in a loss of points. This is a fast-paced exciting round of competition where spectators are encouraged to express their support and encouragement.

The three-man recurve teams shoot at their regular 70 m target while three-man Compound and Bowhunter teams shoot at two regular 50 m (6 ring) targets, meaning there must be three arrows shot at each one. Compound teams shoot four ends of competition with the high score winning the match. Recurve and Barebow teams win two "match points" for each 6-arrow end that they win. If the teams tie an end they each win one match point. The first team to win five match points wins the match. Matches that are tied at the end of four ends will be decided by a three arrow shoot off. If the teams remain tied, the team with the arrow closest to the center of the target wins. Like in the individual competition the one-on-one team competitions continue with one team retiring at the end of each match until four teams are left in each division. With four teams left we shoot the semifinals. At the completion of that match the two losing teams will shoot for a Bronze medal and the two winning teams shoot for the Gold and Silver medals.

The final event of these tournaments is the Mixed Team Round. In this event Mixed Recurve, Mixed Compound, and Mixed barebow teams compete. Each mixed team is made up of one male and one female compound archer from each college while Mixed Recurve Teams are made up of one male and one female recurve archer within their shooting discipline from each college. It's also a tag team event with two archers shooting four arrows in 80 seconds. The event starts with all archers one meter behind the shooting line. When time begins one archer on each team goes to the line to shoot his arrows. Archer #1 shoots one (or two) arrows and leaves the shooting line. Once Archer #1 passes the one-meter line Archer #2 goes to the line and shoots one (or two) arrows and then leaves the shooting line. This continues until both archers have shot their two arrows or until time expires. Like in other team rounds you are allowed to have a coach in a box on the shooting line with the same rules. Archers must be careful to make their exchanges cleanly because if more than one archer or one archer's equipment occupies the area inside of one meter it is a violation. With the first violation, the team receives a Yellow Card. Subsequent violations result in a loss of points. This is a fast-paced exciting round of competition that even allows the spectators a simpler way to keep up with the action. The Mixed Teams also shoot at the same targets as Team Round. Compound teams shoot four ends of competition with the high score winning the match. Recurve teams win two match points for each 4-arrow end that they win. If the teams tie an end they each win one match point. The first team to win five match points wins the match. Matches that are tied at the end of four ends will be decided by a three arrow shoot off. If the teams remain tied, the team with the arrow closest to the center of the target wins. Like in the individual competition the one on one team competitions continue with one team retiring at the end of each match until four teams are left in each division. With four teams left we shoot the semi-finals. At the completion of that match the two losing teams will shoot for the Bronze medal and the two winning teams shoot for the Gold and Silver medals.

Like all tournaments an awards ceremony follows the completion of competition and can include one additional team award that has not been mentioned until now. The overall team champion in these events is the team that performs the best in a combination of all the team rounds and individual competitions in all four shooting disciplines. Scoring for the Overall Team competition is as follows: teams get 10 points for having a team and 10 more points for each team they place ahead of in each category. The Overall Team Champion is the team that earns the most points after tallying all categories of team competition.

This is an excellent tournament format that encourages all schools to develop male and female archers for Recurve, Compound, Bowhunter, and Barebow competition. The more complete your team is the more both the kids and coaches enjoy the competition. If we want to make our sport grow we have got to offer events that the competitors enjoy. Give it a try and you'll be hooked just like me.

**2019 U.S. National Outdoor Collegiate Championships and
World University Games – U.S. Team Trials
Darree Fields – Dublin, Ohio
May 16-19, 2019
Schedule of Events***

Wednesday, May 15, 2019
9:00am – 5:00pm   Unofficial Practice – Practice range open

Thursday, May 16, 2019
11:00am – 3:00pm   **Official Practice/Check-in**
12:00pm – 3:00pm   **Equipment & Uniform Inspection**
2:15pm – 3:00pm   **Team Manager Meeting** – Main Tent
3:15pm – 4:15pm   **Opening Ceremonies**
4:30pm – 7:00pm   **Cookout** – BBQ and Activities Tickets available for pur
                   chase and on-site

Friday, May 17, 2019
8:00am   **Practice** – 3 Ends
                   Qualification Round 1
                   72 Arrows – Recurve @ 70 m; Compound, Bowhunter,
                   Barebow @ 50 m
12:00pm – 2:00pm   **Lunch**
2:00pm – 6:00pm   **Mixed Team Round** – Same as Qualification Distances
6:30pm – 8:00pm   **USA Archery Collegiate Program Meeting** – Location TBA

Saturday, May 18, 2019
8:00am   **Practice** – 3 Ends
                   Qualification Round 2
                   72 Arrows – Recurve=70m; Compound, Bowhunter,
                   Barebow=50m 12:00pm – 2:00pm   Lunch
2:00pm – 6:00pm   **Official Team Round** – Same as Qualification Distances

Sunday, May 19, 2019
8:00am   **Practice** – 2 Ends
                   Individual Elimination Rounds – Same as Qualification
                   Distances 6:00pm – 10:30pm
                   Awards Banquet – Marriott Hotel Ball Room
Please Note Times are subject to change and are approximate. Weather,
Equipment delays and other factors may affect the schedule. We will make
every effort to keep on schedule and notify participants.

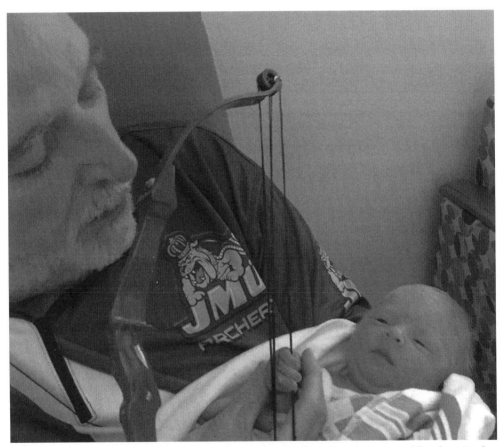

You gotta start'em when they are young! This is me introducing my latest granddaughter, Ryder Randolph to her first bow. She was less than 24 hours old.

3

Keep It Simple

The KISS Principle has been taught since the beginning of time. KISS being the acronym for Keep it Simple Stupid. It seems too obvious to be something that is ignored on a such a regular basis, but it is. The need to give it more attention in my daily life was driven home recently by two separate personal experiences that I would like to share with you in this chapter.

Equipment

College teams are made of the wildest mix of kids you can imagine. When you start practices in the fall you are never sure who or what is going to show up. You have returning team members who didn't graduate off of last year's team. If you are fortunate, you will have a few talented recruits who have chosen your school to have the opportunity to continue their development under your guidance. And then you'll have the really new kids who saw the team's booth on student organization night and always wanted to try shooting a bow. Student organization night at James Madison University has produced as many as 175 new students to the sport of archery in a year and some schools have reported numbers as high as 300 per year. Hopefully, you and your team have a system in place to introduce these new folks to archery in a way that is both fun for all involved and successful in directing the most dedicated and promising students toward the team.

The returning kids are, of course, the stability of your team each year. They have chosen to come back for another year of competition in spite of the fact that they've already met you and worked with you (hopefully you are one of the reasons they chose to return). The point is: they are used to you, your idio-syncrasies, and understand your motivation.

The new kids are the ones I want you to think about right now. These guys are watching your every move and hear everything you say—good and bad.

A couple of months ago at practice I was helping one of the new archers on the team who had decided that he was ready to buy his own bow in the hope of making the traveling team. It is always a very sobering moment when a kid comes to you with $250 in their pocket and is trying to put together a tournament bow set-up just like yours. Well I don't know about the retail prices but I know that my bow with accessories is about $2,000 at dealer cost. So, I spent the next hour building an order for him that gives him everything he needs for around $500 and explaining how little difference there was between the components I was selecting for him and the things I was shooting.

It helped me remember when I was his age I was shooting a bow with a twisted limb that I had bought used for $85 and how I had worked my butt off and won a National Championship with it. Now, I don't shoot as much as I did 40 years ago but when I do I like to shoot good equipment, especially now that I can afford it. The problem is that without knowing it, I was sending a message every time I stood on the line and shot. They were interpreting how I was shooting, score wise, with what I was shooting. Without saying a word to anyone, I made a decision that night. I was going to order a low end set up and start shooting it at practice just to let them know what it could do.

Keep it Simple ... Keep it Positive ... Keep it Growing

I replaced my $750 riser with a $250 riser, my $600 limbs with $80 limbs, my $375 sight with a $20 sight, my $400 stabilizer set up with a $50 stabilizer, my $40 rest with the free one that came with the riser and my $130 cushion plunger with a $25 cushion plunger. I did keep the same tab and the same arrows.

The next week I put the bow together at practice and started shooting it instead of my tournament set up. After a few ends of practice I had my arrows flying and grouping pretty well. My top recurve shooter came over to see how things were going with my new bow and I was lucky enough to shoot a 30. He acted as if he was mad and stomped away saying "Why can't I do that?" I simply replied, "Maybe it's your equipment." The practice room erupted into laughter because he is the only guy on the team with better equipment than I have.

The point is not that you shouldn't waste your money on quality equipment. Far from it. Always buy quality when you can. It will pay off in the long run, whether through performance, ease of use, reliability or simply life expectancy. The point is that everyone has a budget and living within that budget does not mean you can't be successful.

Keep it simple. As long as you choose the right draw weight of bow and the right spine of arrows you can be successful. Naturally, compound bows also need to be adjustable to or set at the correct draw length. It is also important that any bow be set up properly, but once this is done it is all up to you.

Bows are stupid. They do exactly the same thing every time. They don't have independent thoughts and decide to shoot one arrow low, two arrows high and the other three to the right. They will allow you to do that and more; however, they are the most reliable member of your shooting team. So please, if your kids want to shoot better don't just tell them to buy a better bow. Teach them to trust their equipment and perfect their shot. It's just that simple.

Instruction

I recently had an experience where I was not the teacher, I was not the coach, I was simply a student. I found it to be a truly humbling experience. Imagine yourself a student again. You do not choose what to talk about because you are not in charge. Your opinion doesn't matter because you are not the expert. Your experience doesn't matter because it has nothing to do with the topic at hand.

The instructors in this class were very clear from the beginning that only a small percentage of the group could expect to successfully complete the program. As time went on this was reinforced several times a day. While it was clear to me that they were simply trying to make sure that we took seriously the need to work as hard as necessary to learn the concepts, inside and out, the tone was so discouraging that it took a toll on the enthusiasm and openness to new ideas that the group needed to succeed.

I have never found a topic so complex or so difficult that I could not break it down into parts that could be more easily digested.

The results of the tone that was set made many of us wish we hadn't even enrolled in the program. After a few days the stress felt by the students caused several to display medical issues. After seeing and feeling the impact of the tone of this class I determined that no matter how important or difficult a topic was to teach/learn that I would never use this approach. I believe that the effort used to make us give it our all was counterproductive to the overall instructional goal.

I believe whenever you want your students or team members to learn something it is important to Keep It Simple. I'm not trying to suggest that you never have to teach complex or difficult topics. What I am saying is that I have never found a topic so complex or so difficult that I could not break it down into parts that could be more easily digested. I believe that by keeping it simple and presenting all the component parts with a positive approach you can successfully achieve the same learning goal with the positive attitudes and natural enthusiasm of your students intact.

I am thankful for the traumatic experience in that it reinforces for me the importance of being more aware of what I say and how I say it when I am teaching and coaching my team. It's my responsibility to remain mindful that archery will continue to grow and my archers will continue to improve as long as I "Keep it Simple" and Keep it Fun.

It's plain and simple, your students shoot archery because it's fun. And except for the most serious dedicated tournament archers the day they decide archery isn't fun anymore is the day they hock their archery equipment and buy a kayak. So, we accept the role of salesman at the same time we accept the role of coach. By keeping it fun and keeping it simple we sell them every day on shooting competitive archery, or shooting more blank bale or developing a better shooting technique. We never want to introduce a new skill by saying "As important as shooting with back tension is to your success as an archer the majority of team members will never be able to learn this skill . . . and I mean never." If this is your approach to coaching I have only one request. Please change. Change your approach . . . or . . . if you can't change that . . . change sports.

How many times have we spoken in terms that make things sound more complicated or difficult than is absolutely necessary? Remember, it should not be our goal to impress anybody. It should be our goal to engage everybody. When we do that we will have all the time we need to drive home the finer points of the game . . . when the time is right. So when you're trying to figure out what to say:

"Keep it Simple . . . Keep it Positive . . . Keep it Growing"

Don't touch that arrow!
(Electrical circuit breaker shot at 2002 US Indoor leaving the lights on while running a live 240 volts into the arrow.)

4

Insurance
(Don't Leave Home Without It)

Danger! Danger Will Robinson! You are about to travel with your team to their first "away" competition of the year. You will be taking twelve youths to a tournament about 300 miles away for a two-day tournament. You've registered for the event, you've rented a 15-passenger van, you've even gotten certified to drive the big van. Is there anything you've forgotten?

Yes. I believe there is. Do you have a folder in your briefcase with the insurance information for each of the individuals in your care? If not, I suggest you take care of that immediately. While coaching a varsity team at James Madison University I always felt like I was drowning in paperwork. The one pile of paperwork that I didn't resent was the folder of health insurance forms I was required to keep with me on all trips to keep the kids safe.

> *The thing I always dreaded was an accident on the highway where someone needed be taken to the emergency room.*

You never know when one of your kids will fall ill or suffer an injury that requires treatment. But the thing I always dreaded was an accident on the highway where someone needed be taken to the emergency room. When we were traveling with two vans we even made a second copy of the forms so each driver/coach would have a set just in case one van was in an accident and the records were destroyed.

I can't think of anything worse than being responsible for a group of kids involved in an accident, needing medical attention in an emergency room or other medical facility, and not being able to get treatment initiated because I failed to plan for such a catastrophe and did not have appropriate insurance information and authorization to initiate treatment.

Just give the forms out to your team members to complete and only upon return of the completed form are they eligible to travel. When we were a varsity sport, there was no question, until the university got the form back you were not cleared to travel. The coach was not allowed to override the university's requirement.

I have included a sample form for you to use or modify for this purpose. I hope you find this helpful as you plan to take your next team trip.

James Madison University Archery Club
Insurance Coverage Notification Form

Personal Information

Last Name First Name Middle Name		Social Security Number
Campus/Local Address Street City State Zip		Date of Birth
Home Address Street City State Zip		Day Phone

Subscriber
Name & Address of Person providing Primary Accident Insurance Coverage

Last Name First Name Middle Name		Employer
Address Street City State Zip		Day Phone
Social Security Number		Other Phone

Primary Insurance
Attach Copy of Insurance Card (Front & Back)

Insurance Company/Agency	Policy Number Plan or Group Number
Street Address City State Zip	Phone

Authorization for Treatment
Is authorization or physician referral required by your insurance plan to initiate treatment? ___ Yes ___ No If No please initiate treatment. If Yes, for authorization please contact

Individual / Office	Phone	Fax

Emergency Contact Information
Contact should be parent or guardian

Last Name First Name	Relationship
Street Address City State Zip	Phone / Other Phone

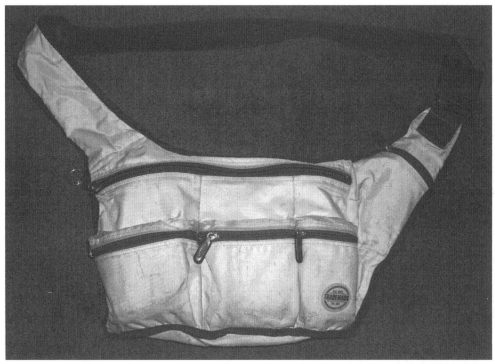

Honest to goodness, this is yellow . . . a faded beat up yellow, but it is yellow. After decades of use it has held up quite well.

5

The Old Yellow Bag
(Being Prepared Isn't Just for Boy Scouts)

Anyone who has attended a major collegiate archery tournament in the last 20 years has probably noticed me roaming the field wearing the "Old Yellow Bag." They've probably also noticed everywhere there is an equipment emergency on the field I seem to appear, digging something out of the Old Yellow Bag, to make the repair and get the archer back onto the shooting line.

I can't tell you how many times I have been asked, "Bob, what all do you have in that bag?" I have always given the simple answer: "Everything." While hardly accurate, it seemed like a much simpler answer than the truth. Now that I'm trying to slow down a little on the coaching side, it may be the right time to answer that question. But before I give you a list of what I carry in that bag I should probably give a little explanation of how it came about.

I started shooting in my backyard when I was a kid, and started competition at the ripe old age of eight. I didn't have a new bow until I was sponsored in college. I made my own arrows and strings and since I didn't have any money, I learned to fix and jury-rig everything else I needed. I have personally experienced more equipment failures during competition than most people could imagine. I have broken risers, limbs, strings, stabilizers, sights, arrow rests, clickers, tabs, nocks and arrows. Having officiated hundreds of events including state, regional, and national championships I never saw an event more prone to equipment failures than the great and historic event, the Atlantic Archery Classic. It was an indoor tournament held at the end of the indoor season at outdoor distances and since everyone was transitioning to outdoor equipment setups and there were 300+ archers on every line it seemed as if there was at least one equipment failure on every end of the shoot.

The equipment failures I experienced as an archer as well as what I observed as an official and then later as a manufacturer's representative led me to understand the importance of being prepared for disaster as a coach. When I was hired as head coach of the JMU Archery Team I noticed most teams traveled with a small fishing tackle box to serve as a first aid kit and most included a few items such as glue, some spare nocks, and dental floss in the kit for minor repairs. Add to my archery experience the fact that I was an Eagle Scout and it was clear that I had to take "the kit" to another level.

The kit I have used has transitioned over the years from a huge tackle box to a rolling plastic tool box and ended up a "Stanley Galvanized Metal Rolling Workshop." This kit is outfitted with every archery repair tool I own along with all the pieces parts I need to keep my entire team up and running no matter what minor repair is required to get them back in the game. Backup bows, limbs, and risers are up to the archers. I make an honest effort to stock The Kit with anything else necessary to prepare me for the unexpected.

The Rolling Work Shop was the first step in my preparedness, but I soon realized while it was mobile it was never going to be where we needed it during a real emergency. Thus, the Old Yellow Bag was born. While the Rolling Workshop could serve as my Field Hospital for all archery calamities, the Old Yellow Bag would be my First Responder Bag. When the team arrived for an event we would set up a central location where we would store our bow cases and the Rolling Tackle Box. The team would go to their target assignments and I would put on the Old Yellow Bag and make my rounds.

The big question is still: "What the heck is in that bag?" While I do change things out once in a while, the approximate contents are listed below.

The Old Yellow Bag

1. Pocket #1 – The Nock Box
   a. Easton Sm Groove G-Nocks (6 ea color)
   b. Easton Lg Groove G-Nocks (6 ea color)
   c. Easton Sm Groove Pin Nocks (6 ea color)
   d. Easton Lg Groove Pin Nocks (6 ea color)
   e. Easton 3-D Super Nocks (6 ea color)
   f. Other nocks in types & colors to match needs
   g. Assorted nock inserts
   h. Extraction tool for broken nocks
   i. Nock Turning Tool (G-Nocks)
   j. Nock Turning Tool (Super Nocks)
   h. Cable Slide
   i. D-Loop Rope
   j. $5/16''$ Nylon & Fiber Washers
2. Pocket #2 – The Screw Box
   a. Dies – $5/16''$ x 24, 10 x 24, 8 x 32

 b. Taps – $\frac{5}{16}''$ x 24, 10 x 24, 8 x 32

 c. Extractors – BX3, BX2, BX1

 d. Recurve Aperture

 e. Tab Ledge

 f. Assorted Launcher Arms

 g. Assorted Points

 h. Assorted Springs

 i. Emery Cloth

 j. Easton Hot Melt

 k. Saunders Nock Sets (5 ea size)

 l. Kisser Buttons (3 ea size)

 m. Assorted Set Screws

 n. Assorted Sight Screws

 o. Assorted Mounting Screws & Bolts

 p. ILF Limb Screw Sets

 q. Assorted Plunger Tips

 r. Assorted Plunger Springs

 s. Toothpicks

 t. Wire Mesh

3. Pocket #3 – The Press Pocket

 a. Bowmaster Portable Bow Press

 b. Bowmaster Split Limb Brackets

4. Outside Pocket

 a. Tape Measure

 b. 3″ x 5″ Cards

5. The Inside

 a. AAE Fastset (cyanoacrylate glue)

 b. Bohning Platinum (solvent glue)

 c. Double Faced Black Foam Tape

 d. Easton Arrow Spine Chart

 e. OMP Ultimate Bow Square

 f. Gloves w/Rubber Grip

 g. 5 Minute Epoxy

 h. Eklind 9 pc Allen Wrench Set (.050, $\frac{1}{16}$, $\frac{5}{64}$, $\frac{3}{32}$, $\frac{7}{64}$, $\frac{1}{8}$, $\frac{9}{64}$, $\frac{5}{32}$ & $\frac{3}{16}$)

 i. Eklind 7 pc Metric Allen Wrench Set (1.5, 2, 2.5, 3, 4, 5 & 6)

 j. Allen Wrench $\frac{7}{32}''$

 k. ViperGrip Vise Grip Pliers

 l. T-Handle for Taps

 h. Blue Loc-Tite

 i. Bohning Excelerator Bowstring Wax & Conditioner

j. Bohning Tex-Tite Bowstring Wax
k. Craftsman Small Multi-Blade Screwdriver
l. Small Utility Scissors
m. Small Needle Nose Vise Grips
n. Klein Electrical Pliers (Cuts Bolts 4/40, 6/32, 8/32, 10/32, 10/24)
o. Small Utility Knife
p. Nock Set Pliers
q. Easton Pro Archery Pliers
r. Small Channel Lock Pliers
s. 6″ Slip Joint Pliers
t. Allway 4 Blade Screwdriver
u. Heavy Duty 4 Blade Screwdriver
v. 2″ Adjustable Wrench
w. 4″ Crescent Adjustable Wrench
x. 6″ Crescent Adjustable Wrench
y. Burris Lens Pen
z. Silver Sharpie
aa. Black Sharpie
bb. Lighter
cc. Dental Floss
dd. Handi String Separator
ee. Leatherman Surge Multi-Tool
ff. BCY Serving Tool
gg. Serving Material
hh. Viper String Loop Pliers
ii. Finger Sling

But, you say: "That's not possible! Where in the world could you get a small shoulder bag that would hold all of that?" Well, sometimes your sacrifices are rewarded in ways you'd never expect. Almost twenty years ago I was accompanying my daughter on a shopping trip to an Old Navy store, having a wonderful time trying to kill time while she carefully inspected every sale item in the joint. As I fondled all the junk they had in the place trying to act interested in the items my daughter was looking at, I casually looked at a yellow shoulder bag. The longer I hung around the more interested I became. Finally, when we checked out I found myself the proud owner of a yellow bag that I hoped I would find a use for.

When I got it home I discovered that the pockets were just the right size for my Plano *MicroMagnum* tackle boxes of nocks and screws. Then I decided that since I could carry vital parts in the pockets I just needed to find a way to carry my tools inside the bag. I went to the hardware store, bought a Bucket Boss Organizer, cut it to into two section to fit the inside of the bag and the rest is history.

Since the Rolling Workshop is the balance of my preparedness formula I have listed its contents below.

The Rolling Workshop

The Rolling Workshop's inventory is pretty much a duplication of the inventory of the Old Yellow Bag plus the following.

1. First Aid Kit
2. Bowstring Kit
   a. Extra Bowstrings (66″, 68″, 70″)
   b. Extra Serving Material
   c. Cable Separator
3. Sight Box
   a. Sight Tape
   b. Recurve Apertures
   c. Scope
   d. Scope Studs
   e. Zeiss Lens Cleaner
   f. Zeiss Lens Cloths
   g. Leupold Lens Pen
4. Tool Box
   a. File
   b. Level
   c. Apple E-Clip Tool
5. Accessory Box
   a. Assorted Tabs
   b. Finger Slings
   c. Wrist Slings
   d. Armguards
   e. Assorted Arrow Rests
   f. Assorted Clicker Blades
   g. Assorted Launcher Blades
   h. Cushion Plunger
6. Point Box (Assorted sizes used by the team)
7. Fletching Box (Assorted lengths & colors used by the team)
8. Adhesives Box
   a. White Lithium Grease
   b. Bow Snot Lube Pen

9. Apple Sight Screw Kit
10. Nock Boxes (additional assortment & quantity)
11. Assorted Screws
12. Assorted Bolts & Studs
13. Propane Torch
14. Bitzenberger Fletching Jig
15. Electronic Grain Scale
16. Arten Arrow Straightener (During Indoor Season)
17. Shop Rags
18. Arrow Puller
19. Arrow Lube
20. Wire Mesh

I believe that if you equip yourself with this assortment of tools and archery accessories that you will be able to solve 99% of the problems your team encounters throughout the season. While I believe most of us could benefit from an explanation of how to handle a variety of crises that our kids will experience the practical application the majority of the items listed in this chapter are straight forward and relatively self explanatory.

Anyone who has a question about what any of the items I have listed are used for or have specific questions about if and how certain repairs can be made in the field are welcome to contact me via email (bowpro1@ comcast.net) and I will be glad to respond.

Note For those who choose to travel light I recommend (at least): a bow square, dental floss, Allen wrench sets (standard/English & metric), fast set glue and a Leatherman-style multi-tool.

And for those of you who can't believe all of that stuff is in the Old Yellow Bag, here are the contents laid out . . . partially anyway.

The 2019 JMU Archery Team posing with the JMU Banner at the Opening Ceremonies of the U.S. National Outdoor Collegiate Championships

6

Finding the Positive

Coaching kids in school offers a rare opportunity to engage them at a time when they are finding themselves and growing into young men and women. Your role as a coach can have a significant impact on the individuals you have the privilege to work with. Please accept your role responsibly and always work to Find the Positive.

Early Training

When you address your group it's important to emphasize the concept that, while nothing comes easy, all things are possible through dedication and hard work. While that often is enough to help them to begin to develop a work ethic it does little to connect with the individuals on a meaningful basis. Each of them understands that comments made to a group do nothing to address their individual strengths, weaknesses, or overall potential. Each individual will need to have one-on-one time with you in order to make a bond and build a relationship of trust and respect.

These relationships start early, so it is important even when working on form before introducing equipment that we find the positive. It can be as simple as saying "Your stance is solid and your posture is great . . . and I need you to relax your hand a little so we can get your anchor under your chin." The first part reinforces what they are doing right, so far, as the second part suggests a correction. All corrections may seem as negatives, that they are "doing something wrong," so mixing a positive reinforcement in makes the correction easier to swallow.

I feel that using humor to keep everyone relaxed during practice is a great thing as long as it doesn't damage a relationship. So after establishing a relationship I may be inclined to correct an anchor with: "What the heck are you doing with your anchor?" while laughing and shaking my head. Then I approach them and help them make the correction.

First Shots

The first shots with a room full of brand new archers can be scary no matter how much prep has been done with mimetics and stretch bands. So find the positive by pointing out and complementing everything that the students do correctly. Try not to miss a single individual in the process. At the end of their first session with bows I like to close out on a happy positive note by saying something like: "Well we survived the first day of weapons training with few self-inflicted injuries. I believe we can build on this." Then I go on to reinforce how well everyone did and finally advise them what we plan to do in the next session.

Training

Every certified coach has been trained to keep a positive approach when instructing and coaching archers so I won't go into any details here except to remind you that the more they learn, the more they will question everything, including their equipment. Make sure they understand the difference between bow/arrow setup and tuning and advise them that their bow is set up for an "average" archer and that you will help them tune it to them when they are able to shoot consistent groups. In the meantime, they need to understand that the equipment is simple and reliable and will do exactly the same thing on every shot. Once they have confidence that their equipment is not causing erratic grouping or occasional fliers they will be much more willing to buy into the fact that they will notice improvements in groups and scores only by becoming more consistent in their shot process. During their development it is important to reinforce their positive skill improvements but it is most important to emphasize how much potential they have for success. My favorite story to share with archers just getting started is about a female archer who shot for JMU in the 90's. As a freshman she only came to practice to watch her boyfriend shoot. As a sophomore she started shooting and made the women's travel team. As a junior she earned All-American honors. Her senior year she won the National Championship and was invited to become a resident athlete at the Olympic Training Center in Chula Vista, CA. This re-emphasizes that with hard work and dedication anything is possible.

When the travel team is selected the only encouragement and positive reinforcement that is needed is for the individuals who were not selected. It is important at that time to let them know that you recognize their hard work and accomplishment and that if they keep working you expect them to make the travel team in the future. Make sure they understand the areas of their game that they need to address to make the needed improvements but be sure to find the positive in the skills that they have already developed and the incredible potential they have.

Continue to be positive in handling each member of the team selected as they prepare for competition. You will face additional challenges when the time for competition comes.

Before Competition

Always plan your travel to the archery venue carefully so that you have your team arrive at least an hour ahead of the start of the event. This will allow them time enough to get their target assignments, establish a team base camp, assemble their equipment and get to their target with 30 minutes to spare. This allows them to stay relaxed while they check out the venue and introduce themselves to their target mates and fellow competitors.

If some piece of equipment has been misplaced, they were given an incorrect target assignment, or any other problem pops up there is time to deal with it without going into panic mode. (You must be the calm at the center of all their storms.) They look to you to resolve their problems regardless of whose fault they are and if you hope to be a successful coach you accept that role positively, without flinching. At a national championship I had one of my best archers tell me that he left his watch in the motel room, 20 minutes away. I asked him if he needed it to shoot and he said "yes." So we jumped in the van and started the drive back the motel. Knowing how heavy his watch was I asked him if he needed it for time or if he used it as a body stabilizer. He acknowledged he used it as a body stabilizer and we both laughed and continued the drive. He went on to win the event.

The point is to do everything to try to keep your athletes cool, calm, and collected before an event. If they get to the event late and have to scramble to get set up in time to shoot, their heart rate will rise along with their level of anxiety bringing down the whole team's performance (as would hearing the coach yelling at an archer for forgetting a piece of equipment or uniform needed to compete). Even if you discover that one of your archers is unable to compete due to an equipment issue, handle it casually and confidently by telling the archer that since he can't shoot today you could really use his help as a team manager for this event. He already feels like a schmuck for letting his team down. Allow him to keep as much dignity as possible by having him fill an important role in support of the team.

During Competition

Have you ever seen one of your archers come unraveled during a competition? Okay, maybe a better question is, have you ever had a competition where one of your archers didn't come unraveled? As coaches, when we see a kid we are working with come unraveled in competition it is one of the most uncomfortable things you will encounter. However you find out about their difficulty, once you know about it, they expect you to be able to fix it. Whether it can be fixed or not, you must maintain that look of quiet confidence that you have developed over the years and listen to them explain their problem. If it is something that you can legitimately resolve you naturally jump right on it, then reinforce the positive strengths in their form and get them back on track. If it is, however, like most meltdowns, not a problem with the 70 m to the target but a problem with the 7 inches between their ears, it will be a more delicate matter.

If this is a younger archer, while reinforcing your confidence in the form he has demonstrated, you can try checking the bow's vital stats (nocking point, brace height, tiller, etc), making a small adjustment and sending him back to the line saying "Your brace height was a little low so I raised it to make it a little more forgiving. Try that and see if it doesn't take care of the problem." This is commonly known as the "Bless the Bow" technique. It often times helps get the archer back on track because while you checked the vitals of his bow he got a little quiet one on one time with the coach, who calmed him down and rebuilt his confidence in his form and was given hope when the coach discovered something amiss with his equipment. All positives. Remember, young archers have to grow and learn so much, we sometimes forget the pressure they put on themselves is almost paralyzing.

If the archer is more experienced, he already knows the problem is with the seven inches between his ears, but he has lost control and is looking for help to resolve the problem. In that case, while maintaining that calm confidence, you look them straight in the eyes and explain that they have allowed the demons to creep into their subconscious mind during their shot process and the only way to chase them out is by using the conscious mind to reestablish his control phrase. Have him use controlled breathing to reduce his heart rate and anxiety level. Then have him visualize his perfect shot, repeat his control phrase, and ask him "Who's in charge?" before he returns to the line. When he responds "I am" he is taking ownership of the plan . . . and while this certainly doesn't heal the wound 100% of the time, it does have a positive impact on their subsequent performance 80% of the time.

After Competition

Archers are often so disappointed in their performance that they don't want to turn their card in to me at the end of the shoot. Some because they shot under their practice average and some because they didn't shoot a new personal best which is always a goal for all of my archers. However, for me, this is the time when I can be most positive about progress and potential. As I sit down with each archer individually to review their cards I simply ask them if they shot every arrow to the best of their ability today. Then I tell them, "All I ever asked of you is to give me all you've got every day." If you did that I am proud of your effort and I promise I will do everything I can to help you get better. (Specifics on how to improve performance through review of scorecards can be found in another chapter in this book entitled "Understanding Comfort Zones.")

Remember you are not only teaching archery, you are coaching young men and women.

Over your career some of your students will see you as a teacher and some as a coach. Some will see you as a friend and others will see you as a mentor. You will have an impact on all you touch and you can only hope that what they get from their time with you will influence them in a positive way. I have been truly blessed to have had the opportunity to coach hundreds of wonderful archers over the past (Oh, my goodness!) . . . 40 years. I've even had a number of archers come up to me years after they graduated and thank me. And when I ask them "What for? I was blessed to have you as a part of the team." One of my archers made me blubber like a kid when he said: "I want to thank you . . . for believing in me when I didn't even believe in myself."

Some of my kids have gone on to be great archers, some to be business and community leaders, but most have gone on to be great people. I am proud of all of them and all of their accomplishments and as for me . . . I will continue forever Finding the Positive.

Patience, Grasshopper

When your kids have learned proper form and have worked hard to try to perfect their shots there will a time when there is a separation of those who start to find success and those who seem to just keep working without any noticeable improvement. When the frustration starts to set in I like to bring things into perspective through the inspiration of the bamboo tree.

I explain that while I want all my kids to be All-Americans in their first year, that I am like the bamboo farmer who plants bamboo shoots each season. The farmer waters them carefully, adds fertilizer, and cultivates the shoots for an entire season with less than an inch of growth to show for his work. He continues the regimen of water, fertilizer, and support for a second season and enjoys more negligible growth the second year. He continues his efforts for two more seasons with no growth to speak of.

Then in the fifth year the shoots finally take root and the farmers can actually watch as the tree grows as much as 80 feet in just one season. The bamboo tree spent four years growing a root system to support the growth to follow. Then I suggest to them to "keep the faith" and "keep on working" because, like the bamboo tree, it takes time to build the foundation needed to perform successfully.

Preparing Your Archers

Here I am coaching a team member in the basics at JMU's indoor facility.

7

Beating Mother Nature
(Getting Your Team Ready for Competition)

The truth hurts. Not all of us are fortunate enough to coach at universities or colleges where sun screen is needed all year round and the only snow you ever see is on TV. The truth of the matter is that most of the collegiate teams in the North and East have to roll right into their outdoor competition with little or no outdoor practice. As a matter of fact in 1973, my Junior year at JMU, we shot just four outdoor tournaments in Virginia, Pennsylvania, and New Jersey in April and it snowed or sleeted at every one of them. It's a cold cruel world.

It is important to understand that my goal for this chapter is to outline a plan to take college students who show an interest in archery in the fall semester to shooting in both indoor and outdoor collegiate competitions in the spring semester. I'm sure you are well versed in how to teach new archers to shoot. What I am going to do is explore things you can do to get them prepared to shoot outdoors in the shortest amount of time.

Here are the steps I recommend:

1. **Organizational Meeting**

   Identify those who are interested in competition and those who just want to play in the backyard. We love them all, but to meet our deadline you will need to focus on those who are at least interested in competition from the beginning. A lot of kids who just come for the fun will end up deciding later that they want to compete. The only problem with that is that they may make that choice too late.

2. **Archery Safety**

   As any archery coach can tell you, with all the freaky, unbelievable, ill-advised things that kids can do when they finally get to shoot arrows out of a bow, "When it comes to Safety . . . There Are No Short Cuts!"

3. **Steps of Shooting**

   a. Mimetics (Without Equipment)

   b. With a Resistance Band

c. With a Bow

I believe you can save some time here by reducing the one-on-one time you would normally have to spend before you can really accomplish anything of value. Once you have introduced the new archers to the steps of the shot you will need them to do some work before they will be ready to continue to the next step. You can issue resistance bands to each of your new archers, appropriate to the bow weight you will be introducing them to. Then explain to them that you will let them shoot once they can pull the resistance band to their anchor 144 times in two hours. This will introduce the new archers to the concept of working independently to accomplish goals. It will also introduce them to the fact that this sport will require effort on their part to accomplish anything.

4. **Shooting Archery**

Take your time here. There is only one way to teach people to shoot, and that's the right way. Plan the work . . . then work the plan.

5. **Developing Archery Skills**

This is another area where you can optimize our time while helping your archers understand their responsibility for their own development. That sounds nice, but how do you pull that off, since at this stage in their development each one of them pretty much needs individual attention in the form of direction and feedback? You can count on doing review of form in groups on at least a daily basis, but in addition to the group review, you will be working with individuals as time allows. About twenty years ago I discovered that there were more of them than there was of me and I decided to post signs on the bulletin board establishing standard practices to provide some guidance for those archers until I could get to each one of them. I started with just one practice on one sign

Practice #1—General

1. Stretching/Warm-Up
   a. 5 minutes
   b. Use stretch band
2. Blank Butt Practice
   a. Distance Optional
   b. Minimum of 2 ends
3. Work on Target Reps
   a. 18 Meters
   b. Three Arrow Ends
   c. Work up to 200 quality shots/day
      i. December 31 Goal 60 Shots/day
      ii. January 31 Goal 90 Shots/day
      iii. February 28 Goal 120 Shots/day
      iv. March 31 Goal 144 Shots/day
      v. April 30 Goal 200 Shots/day

listed as Practice #1 (*left*).

6. **Understanding Equipment**
Naturally, it is very important to begin helping them to understand their equipment at the earliest logical opportunity. I have found that what works best for me is to teach them how the bow, it's various components and the arrows work together, and how the archer can affect these relationships. I personally set their bows up and make minor adjustments to get them to perform better but do not confuse the issue by teaching new archers sophisticated tuning techniques until the time is right. Otherwise they short themselves out, constantly trying to tune their bows before they can even shoot consistently. That effort always proves to be counterproductive. If you want to do them a favor while they are learning to shoot, convince them that they need to have confidence in their equipment because it is going to do exactly the same thing every time. They simply need to focus on themselves in order to improve.

> **Practice #2—Skill Focused**
> 1 Stretching/Warm-Up
>   a. 5 minutes
>   b. Use stretch band
> 2 Blank Butt Practice
>   a. Distance Optional
>   b. Minimum of 2 ends
> 3 Work on Skill Area (as identified by Coach)
>   a. Distance Optional
>   b. Minimum of 3 ends
> 4 Work on Target Reps
>   a. 18 Meters
>   b. Three Arrow Ends
>   c. Work up to 200 shots/day
>   i. December 31 Goal 60 Shots/day
>   ii. January 31 Goal 90 Shots/day
>   iii. February 28 Goal 120 Shots/day
>   iv. March 31 Goal 144 Shots/day
>   v. April 30 Goal 200 Shots/day

7. **Teaching Outdoor Skills Indoors**
   a. *Aiming Off*
   While aiming off is a skill that has little value indoors it can be of great value when you shoot outdoors. Explain to your archers that when they shoot outdoors they will experience changing conditions such as wind and rain. You can't effectively compensate for these changing conditions by moving our sight on every shot. Instead, if the wind conditions cause you to shoot low right blue, you must aim high left blue to compensate. When teaching this skill you must remember that your subconscious mind will constantly try to center the aperture, especially if you shoot an open ring aperture as opposed to a pin or crosshair. The key to teach-

ing someone to successfully learn to hold off is to teach them to pick the spot to aim at to compensate for the drift and then concentrate on that spot while they are aiming. That way, even if they are shooting an open ring their subconscious mind will help them center the aperture around the spot they are concentrating on during the shot.

b. *Simulating Shooting in the Wind*

When you need to teach outdoor skills and you can't get outdoors there is nothing like being able to simulate the condition indoors. You need to install a magical machine that can create wind indoors on demand. Yes, install a big fan you can control with a rheostat. It's been a few years since I have done this personally, but it works beautifully. You can pick up a 42″ Portable Fan that can deliver over 13,000cfm for less than $300. Some units come with variable speed power control but you may need to add a rheostat to vary the wind speed to whatever you want.

8. **Shooting Outdoors with the Comfort of Indoors**

In Korea and all over the world serious competitors are shooting outdoors from indoors, staying nice and toasty while they hone their shooting skills. I have seen more and more dedicated shooting facilities recently where special windows have been installed to allow archers to shoot at outdoor tar-

gets from within the facilities. I envy those fortunate enough to have such a facility, in which to train their archers. So what can we do to enjoy such luxury. Without resources we can't duplicate those conditions but we can take steps to make conditions a little more tolerable. We attend tournaments every weekend during the summer where the host has erected shelters, like carports, to protect archers from sun and rain. These same shelters, erected with three of the optional side panels provide an excellent practice shelter from which to shoot outdoors when the elements are a little too tough for your brand new archers. Setting up a small heat source in the shelter will make for a very comfortable training facility, as long as your archers don't mind walking through the cold to get their arrows. The shelter can be bought for around $300 with portable heaters running another $50. A reasonable investment in the success of your archery team.

Please try some of these ideas this season and let me know what tips you may have to share those of us who share this problem with Mother Nature.

JMU archer Aaron Sackchewsky taking aim at 2019 National Outdoor Collegiate Championships.

8

Aiming to Win

Coaching an archery team is a very challenging endeavor. Much more than coaching an individual, especially if your team ranges in knowledge and experience from complete beginners to nationally ranked archers.

You can never take anything for granted. I recently had a rude awakening when I walked behind an archer who was struggling with her grouping more than her form would lead you to expect. Her elliptical group, left to right, caused me to ask what she was doing with her string alignment. Her reply was, "What's string alignment?" I felt so guilty. How did I let her go this long without teaching her about string alignment? Well, as it turns out, she was not at practice when we introduced string alignment to the rest of her beginners group and I had no record of that.

Then I started thinking how life had changed for me since archery became a club sport at JMU. As a varsity team, I only had to keep up with 16 kids. I developed forms to assess their skill levels and track their progress. Now we carry about 24 on the roster and have 75-150 new students come out for the team each year. Teaching, training. and coaching that many kids with such a wide a range of experience is a skill tracking nightmare. It is hard to remember who has attended which instructional sessions and don't forget, your kids will all develop at different paces which just adds to the fun and challenge.

While this applies to all of the skills you will teach I am primarily concentrating upon aiming in this chapter. When it is all said and done, what do we want our archers to understand about aiming?

Breath Control

Always take at least one deep breath and exhale before the draw process. When you raise your bow arm to the pre-draw position just point your sight at the target and while drawing to your anchor take a more shallow comfortable breath and hold it. This will make sure you keep enough oxygen in your bloodstream and air in your lungs to remain stable throughout the shot.

Approaching the Gold

Make sure your draw always ends up with your sight above the gold. That way you will always start aiming by bringing the sight down onto the ten ring. If you want to test the importance of this trick shoot a few ends coming down on all your shots. Shoot a few pulling up from below and then shoot a few alternating the direction. Then choose the method you find to be the most consistent. It seems easiest to maintain proper grip position and control other variables by always going the same direction, with the vast majority finding their best groups coming when they approach the ten from above.

What Should You See When You Are Aiming?

To aim successfully at the target your eyes will be using items on three separate focal planes. This means you will have to choose which item to focus on.

1. *Target* You should focus on the ten ring. Your eyes should focus so that the target and more specifically the 10-ring will provide the clearest picture.

> *If you are trying to decide how to aim as hard as you can and at the same time execute the perfect shot, choose one. I suggest that you will come out way ahead by executing the perfect shot rather than aiming perfectly.*

2. *Sight Aperture* While focusing on the 10-ring you should aim so that the sight aperture surrounds it, the 10 ring being centered within. The aperture itself will appear slightly out of focus.

3. *String* With the 10-ring centered in the aperture allow the blurred string to simply touch the left edge of the aperture. (Left handed archers should allow the string to touch the right edge.) This is your string alignment. This method of string alignment is not the majority choice so it is important that I explain why I choose it. String alignment is not something anyone wants to spend any time on, including myself. It is for that very reason that I prefer this style. String alignment is something that simply gets taken for granted when you are shooting well and has a tendency to get away from you when you are not shooting well, perhaps the reason. Right handed archers tend to have their string disappear to the right as their form breaks down, they become fatigued and start to turn their heads as they struggle to get through the clicker. By starting with the string alignment touching the aperture on the left side of the aperture, your string actually has to pass across the aperture as things start to breakdown which should set off an alarm in your head and give you an opportunity to put such a shot back on your toe and start again.

Aiming & Execution

Now in a perfect world you will line up target, sight, and string as you start to aim, hold absolutely solid on the 10-ring, execute the shot to perfection and score a ten on every shot. Now I don't want to burst anyone's bubble, but while this is an admirable goal and certainly the picture I have in my mental imagery sequence, realistically the process is slightly more challenging. In the real world, holding that solidly while aiming can only be done with a shooting machine or with your bow in a vise. So we should probably talk about a strategy.

I want to simplify this process for you, so what I recommend is that if you are trying to decide how to aim as hard as you can and at the same time execute the perfect shot, choose one. I suggest that you will come out way ahead by executing the perfect shot rather than aiming perfectly. By working too hard to aim perfectly you will find that while you try to stop all sight movement you will tense up your bow arm and bow hand too much. Since your hands and forearms are sympathetic you will also end up with tension in your release hand and forearm as well. With this method, you will always score worse than you aim. We can solve this problem by allowing your subconscious minds to do the aiming for you while you invest our effort and concentration on executing the perfect shot.

> *To test the importance of this trick shoot a few ends coming down on all your shots. Shoot a few pulling up from below and then shoot a few alternating the direction. Then choose the method you find to be the most consistent.*

That's nice, but how exactly do we get our subconscious mind to do the aiming for us? Well, . . .

1. *Alter the Sight Aperture* The sight aperture I refer to, surrounding the ten ring, works best when altered for this purpose. Most come with some sort of a pin, crosshair, or other configuration in the center of either a round or square housing. I recommend that you carefully remove the pin or crosshair from the center and simply use the empty housing to aim.

2. *Engage the Subconscious Mind* Now that your sight is just an open ring, simply put it on the target and forget about it. Your subconscious mind notices you concentrating on the target with all its concentric rings and sees the sight as just one more ring. Your subconscious mind, requiring order in its universe, will work on its own to line up all the concentric rings while you are taking care of the rest of your business.

3. *Shoot the Float* Once your sight is on the target you will continue to exe-

cute your shot, except that your sight is never absolutely still in the ten. It is always floating in a rough "figure 8" back and forth across the ten. But, it is always returning to the center (your subconscious mind at work). So relax and execute the shot with confidence. Using this method, you will always score better than you aim.

Turning the target face into a funnel to demonstrate the relative ease of scoring well when Focusing More on Execution while Aiming the Float.

I like to use a visual aid when explaining about aiming too hard and aiming with your subconscious mind. I take two 40 cm target faces and cut them from the outer edge at 3 o'clock to the center of the 10 ring. Then I make two cones, taping one with the scoring rings to the inside and one with the scoring rings to the outside. Then I hold up the one with the scoring rings on the outside, pointing the tip of the cone at the archers as if it was their target and explain that when they aim too hard with their conscious mind they tense up too much and when they shoot it will be like trying to land their shots in a ten ring on the tip of a cone. Their mistakes will be magnified and their scores will be lower as a result.

Then I hold up the other target with the scoring rings on the inside, allowing the archers to look into the funnel and explaining that by allowing our subconscious mind to do the aiming we can relax and simply concentrate on executing the shot. This style will always allow us to score better than we aim because of our improved execution.

Coach Ryder turning the target face into a cone to demonstrate the difficulty of scoring well when Focusing more on Aiming than Execution during the shot.

Handling Archers Who Miss Instructional or Training Sessions

I have always been a hands-on, face-to-face coach who likes to see the connection in the eyes of my students. But occasionally, based on circumstances beyond my control, a student will miss a session here of there and miss an important tip. When this occurred in the past, I would track archers' development on the Form Assessment Sheet that I keep on all team members and try to make it up with that archer as time allowed. Steve Ruis, a good friend and fellow coach with a lifetime of teaching experience, shared his technique of dealing with absences. Steve documented the totality of his instructional sessions that he made available to his students for reference should they miss one of his sessions. As a result, I will be developing a similar document and provide handouts or online posts for those who have the terrible misfortune of having missed one of my sessions.

Conclusion

I have attempted to provide information in this chapter that will give coaches and tournament archers alike a better understanding of the process of aiming in target archery but it is important to remember that your scores will improve when you learn to concentrate more on execution and less on aiming.

Now that's a nice group! It was shot at practice but don't expect them to do this in competition if they can't do it in practice and they certainly won't unless they learn how and when to change their sight setting.

⑨
Sight Change Drills

You often find yourself coaching uphill when working with college archers. No matter what your reputation is as a coach sometimes you find yourself preparing a team of relatively inexperienced archers to compete against national champions and other seasoned veterans. This falls under the category of Necessity being the Mother of Invention.

When I took over the JMU Archery Team I had a small group of guys including one returning All-American on the Men's Recurve Squad and just one female archer. I started recruiting on campus for students who were willing to learn how to shoot a bow and compete for JMU. Naturally, anybody we could find with some experience was a big bonus.

We taught most of that team from scratch and as a result I made a considered decision to have the team disappear from fall tournaments. I decided to unveil the team each year in February as the Indoor Season started to heat up. The reasons I made that decision about 20 years ago is that: 1) I didn't want my new archers to shoot in competition until I had had at least four months to work with them and 2) I didn't want them to get used to losing as a team. I wanted time to prepare them and create an expectation of winning.

Naturally, I taught them how to shoot, how the equipment worked, how to shoot in a tournament along with what to do in the case of an equipment failure. All the normal things. We even gave them an introduction into the mental game as preparation for competition. I tried to cover everything they would need to be able to hold their own against the more experienced competition they were about to face.

It only took a few ends in competition to see how I had failed them as their coach. As I walked along the line and saw their groups I would suggest that they change their sights and then I would move on to the next archer. During the event I had to remind them on several occasions to change their sight. As we completed the tournament I had them bring me their target faces along with their scorecards. Ouch! The scores weren't much but the holes in the targets indicated some pretty disappointing group patterns.

The next practice we had quite a talk about the difference in shooting practice and shooting in a tournament. I explained that in practice we don't really need to move our sight all the time because we are working on perfecting our shot more that hitting a 10. In a tournament, "If you didn't bring it with you . . . you're not going to find it there!" so we shoot for score. I asked them why they didn't listen to me and change their sights, and they said that they did change their sights. Most of them made a small change every time I said to. I thanked them and we went on with regular practice, as I continued to think about how to solve this problem.

The next practice I came to I had a plan. My new Sight Change Drill was unveiled that night.

Sight Change Drill #1- Indoors

1. Practice till you are shooting good groups. (Results may vary)
2. Adjust your sight until your group is in the center.
3. Adjust your sight five(5) full turns to the right.
4. Shoot a group.
5. Carefully note the location of the center of the group.
6. Now divide the distance moved by five to give you the amount each turn will move the group. (e.g. $2\frac{1}{2}$ rings of movement by 5 turns = $\frac{1}{2}$ ring per turn) For finer control determine the # of clicks per turn and throw that in the calculations to determine how many clicks to make a specified movement.
7. Re-adjust your sight 5 full turns to the Left to return it to its original position.

Sight Change Drill #2 - Indoors

1. Make sure you are shooting good groups.
2. Adjust your sight until your group is in the center.
3. Adjust your sight three(3) full turns up.
4. Shoot a group.
5. Carefully note the location of the center of the group.
6. Now divide the distance moved by three to give you the amount each turn will move the group. (e.g. 3 rings of movement by 3 turns = 1 ring per turn) For finer control determine the # of clicks per turn and throw that in the calculations to determine how many clicks to make a specified movement.
7. Re-adjust your sight three full turns down to return it to its original position.

Once you have your archers do these drills they will understand exactly how much they need to move their sight to actually move their group. No wasted time, but much more important, no wasted points.

Note All the purists are cringing now thinking how I should be helping them find their shot more than just helping them shoot a higher score by chasing their errors with the sight. I understand that thought completely. However, I am a team coach and my first responsibility is to put my team in a position to win. That means that during a tournament I will help each team member to earn the most points they can with whatever level of expertise they have shown up with at that time. On the following Monday I will become a purist again and try to heal the wounded form that plagued them during the event, but I will not waste precious time trying to heal complex form problems while I watch them sling arrows into the wall during a tournament.

Outdoor Season

The outdoor season brings new distances and new problems. One thing remains the same as during indoor season and that is the need to know how to change their sight at each of these distances. So remember, once they think they have sight settings for each of the distances that they will be shooting, please have them do Sight Change Drills #1 & 2 at each distance for their personal reference. Also, have them record their findings in their personal notebooks along with their equipment's vital information and settings.

Important Note Outdoor Sight Change Drills differ from the Indoor Sight Change Drills in the number of turns to move the sight. Outdoors I recommend changing the windage by three turns instead of five, and changing elevation by two turns instead of three.

Teams often need to prepare for FITA 1440 Rounds or 900 Rounds where they need to change distances during the event. I can't tell you how many times I saw good archers lose tournaments because they lost too many points when they changed distances. Most archers spend all of their time practicing the longest distance in preparation for an event.

I have my team spend a lot of time at the longest distance but a reasonable amount of time at each distance to be shot. One point I drive home with my team that has paid off every year in tournaments like this is that if two equal archers are competing in an event with distance changes the one with the best transitions would win.

With that in mind, I came up with another sight change drill that was invaluable to my team's development. They hated it at first but once they saw the results they were believers in the system.

Sight Change Drill #3 (FITA 1440 Round)

1. Make sure all have sight marks for each distance.
2. Set up targets at all distances.
3. Give them two ends of six arrows to warm up (any distance).

4. Announce "Sight Change Drill"
5. Have them shoot:
   a. 2 Arrows (Men @ 90m, Women @ 70m)
   b. 1 Arrow (Men @ 70m, Women @ 60m)
   c. 2 Arrows @ 50m (Men & Women)
   d. 1 Arrow @ 30m (Men & Women)
6. Have them score their ends and record the location of each shot.
7. Have them multiply their scores to determine their "Tuff FITA Score". The Tuff FITA score is an in-house thing used by our archers to show the importance and impact of dominating at the longer distances. (2 @ 90 m, 1 @ 70 m, 2 @ 50 m & 1 @ 30 m).
8. Have them go directly to the distance(s) they did poorest at and check the mark for that distance.

Once everyone has had 30 minutes to work out their problems we would repeat the drill. It was amazing what a confidence boost each one of the team members got when their "Tuff FITA Score" matched their personal best. They knew when that happened that they were about to give that personal best a good bump in their next tournament.

While it's typical to have recurve shooters post anything from a 5+7 (90 m), 8 (70 m), 7+8 (50 m) and a 9 (30 m) which total 44 which then gets multiplied by to get a Tuff FITA Score of 1,056, the best I ever saw out of one of my recurve shooters was a 9+9, 10, 9+10, 10 for 56 and a TFS of 1,368.

On the compound side you'll see 8+9, 10, 8+9, 10 for 54 and a TFS of 1,296. But the most sobering thing I ever saw on the compound side was 9+10, 10, 10+10, 10 for a 59 and a TFS of 1,416.

Note Modify the drill for the 900 Round by simply shooting two(2) arrows at each of the three distances.

Note As the coach you may observe specific impact patterns during Sight Change Drill #3 that are normally only discovered while tuning with the Eliason/French/Walk Back Method. This would indicate the need for additional tuning, but that will be discussed in another chapter.

Coaches sometimes have to go way too long wondering if anybody is really paying attention and appreciates what you do. But when I caught one of my archers practicing one day and I asked him why he was jumping all over the field, he explained that he had just changed arrows and just wanted to run through the sight change drill to make sure everything was good. It was a small thing, but I smiled to myself and thought "Life really is good."

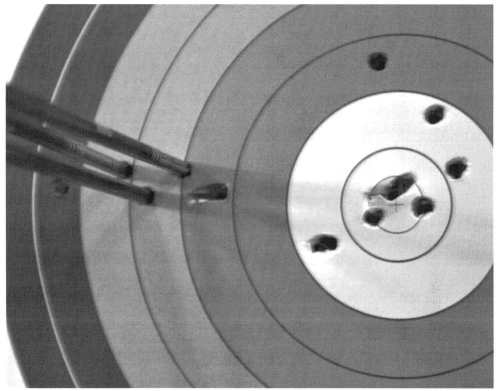

This photo shows a typical result of a sight change drill of five (5) full turns to the right at 18 m. Photo Courtesy of Brad Fiala

Spring practice outdoors, even in the American South, is not without its challenges!

10

Making the Transition to Outdoors

The first year archers that you met in the fall and convinced that it would be fun to shoot archery competitively put their trust in your advice and instruction all the way through indoor season. Now the U.S. Indoor Championships are over and it's time to move outdoors. Don't let them down now.

You have convinced them that shooting indoors is the medicine you take to get to eventually move outdoors where archery becomes even more fun and exciting than shooting indoors. Have you been deceiving them or perhaps you have you forgotten how miserable the first month or so of outdoor practice can be? Oh well, it doesn't matter because as you drag them kicking and screaming into the cold, wet outdoors you get to share the same painful and joyful experiences that will only make them stronger as a team.

First of all, let's think of what they can possibly experience outdoors that they haven't already experienced indoors. While we may experience hurricanes, tornadoes, or tsunamis the Good Lord gave most of us enough brights not to shoot in such conditions. What we very well may reasonably expect to experience in the great outdoors are:
1. Cold Weather . . . Unavoidable . . . We must prepare for the Cold.
2. Wind . . . Unavoidable . . . We must prepare for the Wind.
3. Rain . . . Unavoidable . . . We must prepare for the Rain.
4. Snow/Sleet . . . Unavoidable . . . Prepare as if Cold Rain.
5. Hot Weather . . . Unavoidable . . . Pack your Sunscreen & Suck it Up.
6. Thunderstorms . . . Pack 'em Up . . . Nobody shoots in Lightning.

Now that we have thought of the new experiences we may face when we go outdoors, what preparations do we need to make to deal successfully with these new experiences? These include:
1. Equipment Modifications
2. Clothing Considerations
3. Condition Specific Instruction and Practice
First of all we need to consider the equipment modifications that we will have

to make to improve our odds of success outdoors.

Equipment Modifications

1. *Outdoor Arrows* Since we generally start our new kids out in the fall with light-weight bows and aluminum arrows, at the end of the indoor season we need to get them set up with smaller diameter carbon arrows which will perform better in outdoor competitions, especially in windy conditions. Budgets often determine the arrow choices made here. Everyone would love to be able to afford Easton X-10's, but we have had kids find success with Easton ACG's, Easton ACC's and even the more economical Easton Carbon One. The major problem with shooting the Carbon Ones is the fact that all-carbon arrows are almost impossible to find in the grass with a metal detector and that is a major drawback for beginners.

The shaft diameter difference between indoor and outdoor arrows requires you to consider adjustments to the rest, plunger and nocking point at a minimum.

2. *Centershot* The new carbon arrows that your kids will be shooting outdoors will have much smaller diameters than the fat aluminum arrows they shot indoors and will require adjustments to the position of the cushion plunger to correct their centershot.

3. *Arrow·Rest* The smaller diameter of the new carbon arrows will also require you to raise the arms of the arrow rests in order to place the arrows against the center of the button of the cushion plunger.

4. *Nocking Point* The change of diameter of the arrow also requires you to check your nocking point location and, typically, lowering it slightly to maintain the correct position.

5. *Tuning* I generally try to set their bows up in generally acceptable ranges and wait until they are grouping consistently before we actually tune their bows. Otherwise it's kind of like shooting at a moving target. Once they are shooting with consistent form I will spend the time with them necessary to properly tune their bows.

6. *Sight Settings* Everything up till now could be done in the comfort of the indoor practice room, but getting sight settings requires going outdoors. The first day we go outdoors I explain to the team that moving from shooting at 18 meters to shooting at 70 meters (50 meters for compound) is a process and they are not to expect to do it on the first day. I explain that in an effort to get to 70 meters with enough arrows to compete will require a lit-

tle discipline. The way we do it is to set up targets at 20m, 30m, 40m, 50 m, 60 m and 70 m. The archers all start at 20 m and are instructed to shoot at 20 m till all arrows are in the red and gold. Compound archers are on an 80cm face and Recurve archers on a 122 cm face. Once an archer has accomplished that they are allowed to move to the 30m target. They repeat this process until compound archers are shooting at 50 m and recurve archers are shooting at 70 m. At each distance the sight marks are set for that distance and are recorded.

Naturally team veterans will make it to the competition distances the first day while others may spend two weeks earning the right to shoot at 50 m or 70 m. But once they are there they will still have most of their arrows and they'll be starting to feel a little better about themselves and this thing called outdoor competition.

Now it's time to talk a little more about preparing for the conditions we may face outdoors. You have made an effort to give them good instruction, good advice, and good coaching up to now. You have gained their trust so far, let's not blow it now. They are following you into the cold, wet out-of-doors and it may be appropriate to try to give them some guidance in comfort and survival.

In addition to the changeover of arrows and adjustments to centershot and rest position, we need to take into account a changeover into appropriate clothing. Your kids, if anything like mine, are not prepared to shoot in miserable conditions without a little guidance from you. Your experience will be invaluable in making the transition to outdoors without losing a number of archers because if you are miserable your are probably not having fun. And if you're not having fun . . . what's the point?

The kids show up to the first outdoor practice in winter coats, thinking that they are going to shoot. Well, how well do you think that's going to work? We better get started because there is no time to waste.

Clothing Considerations
Conditions = Perfect

Footwear Your shoes are a little talked about accessory in the sport of archery but I can assure you that they are important and require some consideration. You should try to shoot in shoes that are both comfortable and stable. You want your shoes to be comfortable because if your feet hurt it's hard to concentrate and maintain your focus on the task at hand. You need your shoes to be stable because a consistent stable stance starts with a proper stable foot position maintained in even difficult footing by wearing stable footwear.

I'm not suggesting that you go buy a pair of special German-made *Sauer*

Shooting Shoes used by athletes from around the world in a much louder shooting sport. Many serious archers shoot in boots for this reason. No matter what they are standing on, the footing seems stable. When you try on your shoes, how much movement do you have side to side? A firm sole is recommended as well as a solid heel cup. Firearm shooting shoes had plywood or unbending leather soles until they were outlawed requiring the sole to flex similar to the flex of the human foot. Indoors the footing was perfect and provided stable footing in spite of the footwear chosen. Outdoors you will find many more variables and thus the need for stability in your footwear. Personally I found a Red Wing Shoe that works well for me. Just remember, when they seem well broken in it may be time to shop for a new pair.

Shooting Top Your selection of clothing for your shooting top in perfect conditions is very simple. It just needs to fit properly and pass the dress code for the event or governing body. All I really mean about fit is that there is no loose or bulky clothing that your bowstring can strike and the shirt or top is comfortable to wear. Many shooters have adopted the use of dri-fit shirts that fit the contour of their bodies. These high tech shirts provide comfort in the heat by wicking moisture away from the body where it is easily evaporated allowing the wearer to stay cool and dry. These same shirts can serve as a sweatbox if they are baggy because instead of wicking they trap the moisture inside and simply act like an oven.

Shooting Bottom Your primary responsibility in perfect conditions is to simply meet the dress code. Slacks, skirt, shorts, skorts and kilts are allowed in most events as long as the length of the shorts, skorts and kilts do not cause an uproar. The idea is to just be comfortable without making other people uncomfortable.

Shooting Hat While a lot of archers don't wear hats at all, with all the skin cancer that's being diagnosed, I believe it is my responsibility to recommend a hat that provides some protection from the sun. You simply want to select a hat with a short enough brim to allow string clearance at full draw and wide enough to provide some protection to your face, ears and neck. Since I am fortunate enough to still have a thick head of hair I like a hat with a solid top, mesh sides and solid brim.

Conditions = Cold

Footwear To keep your feet comfortable in cold weather simply requires a little insulation. Whether you choose an insulated shoe or boot or a nice wool sock it is important to consider the temperature before you arrive at the event unprepared. Thinsulate™ is an excellent low bulk insulation used in shoes, gloves, and other clothing items. Another method some people use to keep their feet warm in competition is using foot warmers. They are just like the hand warmers in that you shake them up and they get warm. One caution though, please do not accidently put hand warmers in your shoes. They get too hot and have actually caused burns in some cases.

Shooting Top It's all about the layers. You want to start off with perform-ance underwear that keeps you warm and wicks the moisture away from your skin. The outer layer should be a close fitting performance jacket that is both insulated and waterproof or at a minimum windproof. Depending on just how cold it is you may wish to work one more layer in between these that may be fleece or something else with enough loft to provide insulation. It is important to make sure the outer layer provides you the clearance you need to be able to shoot your bow without any interference with the bowstring. One way to make baggy outerwear more form fitting is with bag clips, Velcro strips, tape, or rubber bands.

Shooting Bottom Start off with performance underwear and top that off with a pair of pants that can also perform wind proofing duty.

Shooting Hat When it's cold I resort to a leather hat that allows me to retain body heat better than a baseball cap. Depending on how cold it is will determine whether you need an insulated hat with insulated ear flaps or muffs.

Other In bitter cold, without insulation, your fingers will slowly lose their ability to perform fine motor skills and you will eventually no longer be able to nock your own arrows on the string. Welcome to the beginning of hypothermia. To prevent your kids from having this experience and having to go up and down the line snapping arrows onto their strings give them hand warmers. If you have contacts with a football team you can borrow the team muffs that all the skill players who handle the ball wear. It's an insulated tube mounted on a belt that you can wear in the front or the back that you can stick one hand in each end to keep your hands warm. Its even better with a couple of hand warmers stuffed in there. There are also hand warming muffs avail-able in most bowhunting stores. You will want two because you wear them on your hip for your release hand but on really cold days your bow hand will want one too. Naturally, their performance is also enhanced with the use of hand warmers.

Please take the time to treat all lenses, both on spotting scopes and shoot-ing scopes, with an anti-fog treatment or spray prior to any tournament. Also, it's important to remember that a lot of the fog that you experience on your scopes is when the temperature is making a big change. For example, if you keep all your scopes in the warm motel room overnight, then go to the field where it 42 degrees all the glass in all your scopes will fog initially at least until they reach air temperature. The anti-fog treatment should prevent minor fogging that you may have experienced in the past and will greatly reduce the total fogging that occurs with temperature shock.

Conditions = Rain

Footwear Shooting in a warm rain some archers choose to do nothing to keep their feet dry and just end the day with funky swamp feet. Personally, I've gone the funky foot route before and now choose to keep my feet dry and comfortable by wearing a waterproof shoe/boot. While there are many names of waterproofing used by different manufacturers Gore-Tex™ is the most time tested and universally accepted name in waterproofing systems. I have used a lot over the years and my favorite shoe right now is the Merrill *Moab Waterproof.* They provide a stable foundation and while they are waterproof they are also breathable allowing my feet to remain dry and comfortable in all conditions. If your kids are like mine, though, some of them will buy the best of everything while others are broke like I was in college. In the latter case there is nothing wrong with shooting in stable rain boots, slipping rubbers on as an overshoe solution and if you don't have rubbers we have even used plastic bags and rubber bands successfully to do the same thing.

Shooting Top A form-fitting rain jacket that provides proper string clearance is what you should be shooting in in a warm rain. That being said when I was in college and many times since, I chose to shoot in my regular shooting shirt and slacks in a warm rain. It was comfortable when I put it on and I never had a clearance problem.

A cold rain is an entirely different story. You will want to combine the information provided in the "Cold" section (above) with the need for a top layer that is both form fitting and waterproof to provide you the protection you need. Under this category, necessity is the mother of invention, I carry boxes of tall kitchen bags and larger trash bags for emergency rain gear. I have the kids put on that first layer, performance underwear or a long-sleeve tee shirt and an optional second layer of insulation. Then I cut head holes and arm holes in the plastic trash bags and have them put them on next. We then have them put on a form fitting outer layer over top of the trash bag leaving the bottom of the bag hang out over their pants helping to keep some other parts warm and dry as well. Yes your arms will get wet and cold but your core will be warm and dry and clearance should not be a problem.

Shooting Bottom Basically, in a warm rain your choice is to shoot in what you are wearing or put on a pair of rain pants. Fit doesn't matter here so it is a much easier solution. If it is a cold rain I recommend you wear a pair of pants or insulated underwear or both on under the rain pants.

Shooting Hat The purpose of a rain hat in archery competition is simply to keep the water out of your eyes while you shoot. If your are shooting in a cold rain them you also want your rain hat to be insulated to keep your head warm and dry in addition to keeping the water out of your eyes. I recommend a Gore-Tex™ hat with a short brim all around and while Gore-Tex™ rain suits are expensive a simple Gore-Tex™ hat is a relatively inexpensive purchase.

Other Try to keep your hands as warm and dry as possible under the conditions. Make sure you keep a towel in a bag to dry your hands as necessary. You can't have enough towels, waterproof stuff bags, plastic trash bags or Ziploc bags at a rainy tournament. You'll want to cover all your scopes with plastic using duct tape to hold it in place with overhang over both optic and objective lens. It won't keep them from fogging up but we have to keep as much water away from the optics as we can. The anti-fog treatment that we did for cold weather will also help with some of the fogging associated with rain.

Always try to wax your bow string when it needs it but especially before a tournament where you may experience rain. Another thing you might want to do before a rain event is to oil or spray all exposed metal parts with WD-40 to both lubricate and protect from rust and corrosion. If you forget to do it before the rain, make sure you use "canned air" to blow the water out of the releases, binoculars, sights, etc afterwards. Then make sure you treat them later, once everything is clean and dry again. While scorecards are generally served to you in large Zip-Loc bags in a rainy tournament it is still sometimes helpful to have an umbrella to help with scoring at the target in the rain.

Hopefully these few notes will help you think about how to help your kids to transition to the Great Outdoors.

Coaches Eye on an iPad with an edited image of Daniel Suter at full draw.

11

The Coaches Eye

Once in a blue moon something comes along that can change the way we do things. Right now I would say that I have found something that is changing the way I do things: *Coaches Eye*, this is the single coolest coaching tool I have ever seen.

For only US$4.99, only half the price of a tube of glue, your coaching can take a leap into the 21ˢᵗ century. Coaches Eye is an app designed to operate on your iPad, iPhone, iPod Touch and even Android devices with a rear facing camera running 4.0.3 or better.

As far as I'm concerned, this one app makes the purchase of my iPad worth every penny. While you can use it on your mobile phone the iPad is the perfect platform and, due to its size, clearly provides the best results. If you have an iPad, I do want to suggest one additional purchase to make this new tool easier to use. The purchase I'm referring to is the New Trent *Grabbit Case* for the iPad, which allows you to comfortably hold the iPad with one hand while videoing your students and immediately analyzing the videos right in front of them.

Many coaches have invested thousands of dollars in video cameras over the years to record the form and progress of their student archers. Some have invested thousands more on video playback units that had slow motion capabilities and other special features to be able to show their students what they are doing and coach them to better form.

The Coaches Eye allows you to quickly and conveniently record your archers, then immediately play the recording back for them. In addition, you have the capability to analyze the video with notes and drawings on the video right on the spot. It is great to be able to provide immediate feedback to your archers allowing them to make changes, be re-recorded and be able to see the new video to see if they are on the right track.

Another feature I enjoy is being able to take videos of archers during a league night without providing immediate feedback. Instead, I can take the iPad home and analyze the videos at my leisure before providing any feedback. When analyzing the videos, Coaches Eye provides a wide variety of opportunities. The easiest of all is to simply share the unedited video through email, text messaging, Facebook, YouTube, or Twitter.

Getting Started

The first step is to select one subject from your team whom you've worked with before and preferably with whom you have mutual trust and respect because, for a change, he will be helping you learn. In a quiet setting, video your subject shooting from an angle and a distance that gives you a view that you would like to analyze. I used, as my subject, Daniel Suter of JMU, the 2012 Collegiate World Champion in the Men's Compound Division. I first took a video of Daniel as he went through the process of finding the right anchor for the new release he was learning to shoot. We made the mistake of commenting on what we were doing as I took the video. I then played back the video for Daniel and we discussed the pros and cons of the different positions. Before I left practice, I emailed the video to him for his personal review. After I went home that evening I made my first attempt at analyzing a video. I opened the app, chose Videos, selected the Video I wanted to review, chose Analyze from the menu, pressed the Record Button at the top of the screen, pressed the play button and when the video started I noticed that the talking back and forth that Daniel and I did made it more difficult to get a quality audio recording of the Analysis. As a result on my next attempt, I simply played the video to the anchor that I wanted to discuss, used the flywheel to select the frame of the video that was perfect for comment and performed an Analysis of my first video on a single frame. I hit the record button, started commenting on the anchor, drew on the video while I commented, and hit the record button again when I was done. When I played this recording back I decided it was a fair representation of what I wanted to say and I emailed it to Daniel.

Daniel in the meantime was so excited about the new tool we were using that he went home and downloaded the app for his Android phone. He then went on YouTube, found video of Reo Wilde shooting in a World Cup competition, shot a video with his phone from his computer screen and then imported it into the Coaches Eye app. Once there he selected the video that I had sent him, selected Analyze Video, tapped the side by side button and then chose the video he had imported. At that point he simply advanced each video separately till they were at exactly the same position in the shot sequence and then zoomed to make the images the same size. All he had to do then was to advance each video frame by frame to study the differences in the movement in the process to complete the shot.

I have since discovered that if you would like to use other videos with Coaches Eye you can import those recorded in certain formats (.MP4, .MOV, .M4V or Android .3GP and .MP4) into the free app, "Dropbox," a file sharing app, and from there gain access to them for analysis with Coaches Eye.

This app has impressed me so much that I look forward to being able to develop archers for competition at JMU in less time and with more solid results than in the past. I will be able to maintain a library of all of my archers as they develop while providing each team member a copy of their own videos. In addition, I plan to collect videos of other top archers which I can share with my archers in a simple email. They will be able to study them at their leisure as the motivation hits them.

The videos are so economical and so easily shared I am also inspired to record instructions on a variety of topics. Often I find that when I make an instructional presentation to the team it is difficult for everyone to see the details. Other times the team members I really intended to reach are not in attendance for one reason or another. If I record videos of these presentations no matter how simple, I can place them in the team library making them available for viewing at their convenience. When a new team member is ready to fletch arrows, all he has to do is pull up the video on their phone and get instructions on how to fletch those first arrows. If they are ready to tune their bows they can pull up the tuning video and make sure that they follow the right procedures and take the steps in the right order.

I apologize if I sound too enthusiastic for an old guy, but this is the most exciting toy I have played with for a long, long time.

I don't care if you are an old coach, or a young coach, or just an archer looking for an advantage, this tool is worth the trouble. Please give it a try and let me know what you think. Feel free to send along any hints you think that I might like to try. You can contact me through email at bowpro1 @comcast.net. I'd love to hear from you.

Coaches Eye – A Simple Start Up Guide

For those of you who are interested the Coaches Eye I have outlined below how to use it for the first time along with a description of some of the features.

1. Open App

  a. Touch the Coaches Eye Icon on your device
2. Take Video
  a. Select Camera (Touch the Camera)
  b. Aim the Camera (Frame the Subject in the Screen)
  c. Start Recording (Touch the Record Button)
  d. Record the Video (Maintain the Subject in the Screen)
  e. Stop Recording (Touch the Record Button)
3. Analyze Video
  a. *Select Video* (Touch the Video you wish to Analyze)
  b. *Select Analyze* (Touch the Analyze Button)
  c. *Plan Analysis* (Touch the Play Button to watch the Video first, take notes and develop a game plan)
  d. *Analyze Video* (Touch the Record Button – At this time it will begin recording your voice but the video itself will remain paused until you choose one of the tools for speed of play)
    i. Speed Tools
      1. *Play* (Touch the Play Button to play the Video at regular speed)
      2. *Slow Motion* (Touch Slow and then Play to play the Video in slow motion. If you only wish to play a portion of the video in slow motion Touch Play and run until the portion you wish to slow down and then Touch Slow. When you want to return to regular speed just touch Slow again.)
      3. *Fly Wheel* (Located at the bottom of the screen this tool allows you to advance at high speed with the flick of a finger, scrub back and forth the find a specific spot to analyze or simply advance the video one frame at a time for the greatest detail)
      4. *Combination* (You have the ability to use the tools for speed in any combination and in any order)
    ii. Drawing Tools
      a) *Box* (Used to bring attention to a portion of the video, easily sized and comes with 5 color choices)
      b) *Circle* (Used to identify a specific point of focus in the video, easily sized and comes with 5 color choices)
      c) *Straight Line* (Used to point out alignment, etc, also comes in 5 colors)

       d) *Freestyle Arrow* (Used to bring attention to a specific point in the video, 5 colors)

       e) *Freestyle Line* (Used drawing any shape or object for the analysis, 5 colors)

       f) *Undo* (Clears the most recent drawing made in the analysis)

       g) *Redo* (Returns the most recently cleared drawing)

       h) *Clear* (Clears all drawings made in the analysis)

       i) *Zoom* (Double tap a section of the screen to Zoom in or use the pinch technique to change zoom with the movement of two fingers)

    iii. Split Screen

       1. After selecting a video to analyze touch split screen and you will be prompted to select a second video to analyze or compare for study.

4. Share Video

   a. Select Video

   b. Sign In

   c. Choose

The New Trent iPad Case as recommended above ... and no, I am not a paid spokesperson for this doohicky.

Two Super Dukes, Shaun Harbison and Andrew Knoll, prepare to defend fair competition at an archery tournament. I felt safer immediately.

12

Don't Forget to Play Defense

It was the best of games, it was the worst of games, but what it really was and still is . . . is my favorite game. One of the things that drew me to archery as my lifetime sport is the genuine good sportsmanship of the wonderful individuals who I have had competed with over the years. Generally speaking, almost everyone I have had the opportunity to interact with in archery has been honest and fair and would not take advantage of another archer's inexperience, weakness, or mistake for their own benefit.

If you have seen a track meet you have probably seen competitors running the track when one stumbles and falls on the track and the other runners just run right past knowing they are one step closer to the podium, some even angered that they had to run around his body sprawled out on the course. In archery, if an archer suffers an equipment failure fellow competitors spring into action to provide assistance by helping the archer to make the necessary repair or even loaning them their own back up equipment. All of this just to keep one of your competitors in the game. This is what I have always done in tournaments and this is what I want my team to do when faced with the same opportunities.

Another thing I like to teach my team before their first real competition is the importance of playing defense. While 99% of the people you will run into in our sport are perfectly honest, there is always that one guy who values winning more than his own character and reputation.

So how do you play defense in an archery tournament? Your archers must understand how the game is played and where people are most likely to gain an unfair advantage.

For example, target archery has rules covering how scoring is to be done and if followed the abuses are few and far between. When you receive your target assignments at a tournament each person on the target has a specific responsibility:

Archer A – Call all arrows ...

If unable to make a call Archer A will ask for assistance from his target mates. If no consensus is reached or if Archer A's call of an arrow is challenged, then Archer A shall appeal to the closest Judge for the official call. There are no further appeals.

Archer B – Scorer #1

Archer C – Scorer #2 ...

As scorekeepers Archers B & C are responsible for making sure each scorecard is properly marked to clearly identify the correct archer, placing the scorecards in the order their arrows are to be called, recording the correct arrow scores legibly onto the correct locations on each card, accurately adding all scores etc, totaling all columns and filling all appropriate boxes after shooting is complete for the day, then signing the completed card and securing the signature of each target mate. Then Archers B & C shall give the fully executed cards to the individual archers for them to sign and turn in at the scorer's table.

Archer D – Observer...

As observer, Archer D is responsible for making sure Archer A's calls are correct and made in the correct order for the Scorekeepers. He is also responsible to check the Scorekeepers from time to time to make sure they are recording the correct values and are recording on to the correct score card. Note In many tournaments you are allowed to trade responsibilities with your target mates as long as all agree.

> While 99% of the people you will run into in our sport are perfectly honest, there is always that one guy who values winning more than his own character and reputation.

While this is the formal plan that is set in place for target tournaments, most of the time the archers on the target will simply decide amongst themselves who calls and who keeps score. Often, an archer will offer to call arrows if somebody else agrees keep score. Anytime an archer volunteers to call all the arrows the first red flag goes up. Keep in mind, on this first red flag it probably means nothing more than the fact that he prefers not to be saddled with having to keep up with the score cards. The point is that this is the position that provides the majority of opportunities to alter the outcome of the event.

The next red flag goes up when the scorer rushes up to the target before the other archers get there. While he may simply be checking to see if he has any close calls prior to scoring the arrows he may be making a plan.

Red flag number three goes up if you notice that his calls are "generous" either for everyone's close arrows or only his. Most people don't mind if some-one gives them the benefit of the doubt on a close arrow but some people give the benefit of the doubt on all the close arrows knowing that they won't ques-tion when they give the benefit of the doubt to themselves. Sometimes the benefits can be pretty generous and if you think about it a little, you'll realize that while he may be treating you the same that he is treating himself, you are both cheating everybody else in the tournament, because they aren't using the same relaxed scoring method.

" Your archers must under-stand how the game is played and where people are most likely to gain an unfair advantage. "

If his generous calls seem to be focused primarily on his own arrows then Archer D should challenge the call. If Archer D won't challenge the call then it falls to one of the scorekeepers, Archer B or C. If he changes the call then all is well and you'll just need to keep an eye on him the rest of the round. If he doesn't change the call then you have a disagreement and need to call a judge for an appeal.

So, what is the correct way to score an arrow in the target? First of all it's not the hole that is scored, it is the arrow, and the arrow is scored where it lies. If an arrow is close, looking down the shaft of the arrow is not the best way to check. It is preferred to look at it from two angles closer to the face of the tar-get. If you determine that the arrow is touching the line, or where the line would be if it were undisturbed, then the arrow counts the higher value. Always call arrows in this way, and once the call is made, if there is a dis-agreement with the call, then and only then do you call a judge for an appeal.

A huge red flag goes up when the archer calling the arrows pulls his arrows as he is calling them or immediately after calling his last arrow. In a formal event he would have to score his arrows last to accomplish this since you are not allowed to touch the buttress or the arrows until they are all scored. In an informal event, he might choose to call his arrows first allowing much less time for observation.

We have to make sure that our newer archers aren't going to be intimidat-ed by older or more experienced archers when they find themselves in a situ-ation like this. If you don't address this topic with them they will be unlikely to even catch what is going on. Nobody wants to be the bad guy and call some-one down for cheating. That's why it's important during the tournament to do your job consistently, all the time, making it hard for a cheater to get away with generous calls from the beginning. Dispute a call early in the contest and you set the tone for what you will tolerate and what you won't.

> *A huge red flag goes up when the archer calling the arrows pulls his arrows as he is calling them or immediately after calling his last arrow.*

While everything I have discussed above applies to both indoor and outdoor competition, the one additional trick I have seen outdoors is the dreaded Silent Mulligan that has been around for at least 40 years. This generally occurs on a target with skilled archers who seldom miss the target. One of the archers is caught by a gust of wind and ends up shooting a miss. When after scoping the target he finds no evidence of the shot, glances behind himself to see if anyone saw the shot and then decides to take a chance on shooting another arrow. When he gets to the target he doesn't even bother going behind the target to look for the arrow in hopes that his action goes unnoticed. You can't watch everyone shoot every arrow but one way to protect yourself is to make a mental note of how many arrows each archer keeps in his quiver. If you notice a lower count when you get to the target take a brief glance behind the target or suggest that Archer D should check for any lost arrows. If none is found just assume everything is okay. Lest you think I am paranoid, I have been made aware of this happening at both a World Target Championship and at a U.S. Olympic Team Trials.

Hopefully, you and the members of your team will never experience anything like the scenarios I have outlined above and the real value of this chapter will simply be to explain 1) Archers Scoring Responsibilities and 2) How to Call an Arrow. Either way, you and your archers are better served being aware of what can go on.

*Team round excitement as JMU's Men's Recurve Team wins the
National Outdoor Collegiate Team Championship.*

13

The Team Round – Part 1
How the Team Round Works

Coaching college archers is often very similar to teaching or working with any other group of archers trying to have fun while working to get better. One event that I have found makes this experience different and more challenging is the Team Round. While you can make it as simple as just explaining how the Team Round is shot and making sure you have the right number of kids on the team, I prefer to be a little more creative.

First of all, to be able to prepare our teams for the competition we must understand the rules of the team round and how it's shot. While I will explain the basics of how the team round is shot I encourage you to become familiar with the complete rules for Team Round Competition and for that I refer you to the FITA Rule Book 2, Chapter 7-Outdoor Rounds which is available online for free at http://newrulebook.ianseo.net/PDF/EN-Book3.pdf.

In an effort to eliminate confusion I will start out by writing specifically about the Team Round for Recurve Archers and will address any minor differences for Compound Teams at the end of the chapter.

The Team Round (At Least the Basics)

The Team Round for Recurve archers is shot at 70 m at the regular 70 m target face while for Compound archers it's shot at 50m at their 50 m "6-ring" target face. The round is basically a tag team event with three archers shooting six arrows in two minutes. Each archer shoots two arrows during that time frame in any order they choose.

I need you to picture the field now. Your team is on Target #1. A One Meter Line has been added for the Team Round, located one meter behind the shooting line. The event starts with all three archers behind the 1-meter line. Archer #1 can only cross the 1-meter line after the Director of the Shoot (DOS) starts the match and the time clock. The archer can only draw an arrow from his quiver once he is on the shooting line. If the archer crosses the 1-meter line early or draws his arrow before he is on the shooting line the judge will raise a yellow card requiring the archer to retreat behind the 1-meter line to start again or be replaced by another archer. If the archer fails to obey the yellow card and shoots his arrow without starting over he will receive a red card from the judge and the team will lose its highest scoring arrow of that end.

Archer #1 will typically shoot his two arrows and promptly retreat behind the 1-meter line. Once Archer #1 and his equipment have cleared the 1-meter line Archer #2 can cross the 1-meter line, step onto the shooting line and shoot his arrows. Once Archer #2 and his equipment has cleared the 1-meter line, Archer #3 can cross the 1-meter line and shoot his arrows. It is important to note that the archers have the option of shooting one or two arrows at a time in any rotation as long as they shoot all six arrows in the two minutes allowed. Each match in the Team Round is a maximum of four ends of six arrows. Compound teams shoot four ends with the high score winning the match. Recurve teams shoot a set system where they earn two "match points" for each 6-arrow end they win. If the teams tie an end they each win one match point. If there is a tie at the end of four ends, recurve or compound, the teams will shoot a tie breaker. Each team will have one minute to shoot three arrows, one arrow per archer, and if the score remains tied, the team with the arrow closest to the center wins. As in other single elimination events, the winning team advances while the losing team is retired.

Teaching the Team Round

How do you teach your team to shoot the team round? Here is how I do it.

#1 Get them comfortable shooting the distance. Obviously if you're going to shoot a team round at 70 m you need to get your team used to shooting the distance as soon as possible. If your team is a group of veterans this is not necessary. However, if you are teaching new archers with little or no competitive experience they may suffer some serious growing pains when they move from 18 m to 70 m for the first time . . . and it's a cold cruel world, in the North and East Regions in particular, that expects a brand new collegiate archer to be ready to compete outdoors at 70 m just thirteen days after shooting the U.S. Indoor. I like to start them out at 20 m outdoors with a rule that if they shoot them all in the red they can move back 10 m. They make the move as individuals rather than a group and simply continue that until you get them all to 70 m.

#2 Get them used to shooting the timing. First, if you've got new kids it can be fun just getting them used to shooting with a timing light. It is another authority figure who can take things away from them without apology. It's

a harsh reality for a kid who got into shooting archery because it was fun and relaxing.

Now that he has figured out how to cope with shooting his three arrows in two minutes we sneak up on him and tell him that in the team round he is going to have to tag team with two team mates to shoot a combined six arrows in those same two minutes. Initially panic can set in. All you have to do is to convince them that one thing that all successful archers have learned to do is to shoot aggressively. Not fast, not rushed, not hurried . . . just aggressively. They need to execute their shot, just the way they've been taught. Not faster, just with a more aggressive mindset. They learn to avoid any stalls or hesitation they may have built into their shot when learning how to shoot a good shot. Initially we taught them to slow down, not to snap shoot and not to shoot so fast as we teach them control and proper execution. Then later in their development we find ourselves teaching them to shoot faster by asking them to shoot more aggressively and helping develop a sense of urgency in the execution of their shot. This pays dividends in not only the team round but all the competitions they will enter in the future.

#3 Teach them how to shoot the team round. Over the years I have seen some pretty ugly team round execution. But what do you expect since we seem to let every group of three archers who participates in the team round come up with their own plan. Come up with a plan and teach it to each of your teams and save them the pain of learning by trial and error.

This is the simple plan I teach.

1. There are three archers – Archer #1, Archer #2 and Archer #3.

2. There are 3 positions – Position #1 Shooter, Position #2 On Deck & Position #3 Spotter

2011 JMU Team Round Practice - (L to R, Archer #1 Bryan Brady - Shooter, Archer #3 Scott Einsmann - Spotter, Archer #2 Adam Stone - On Deck) Photo Courtesy of Brad Fiala

3. Each Archer must dedicate himself to doing the best job he can in fulfilling the responsibility of the position he is in.
4. Start the team round with Archer #1 in Position #1, Archer #2 in Position #2 and Archer #3 in Position #3.
5. When you hear two blasts of the whistle all archers prepare to perform their role but no one crosses the 1 meter line.

6. When you hear one blast of the whistle the timer starts with two minutes on the clock.

   a. Archer #1 crosses the 1 meter line, steps onto the shooting line, draws an arrow from his quiver and starts his first shot.

   b. At this time Archer #2 must:

      1. Be ready to go to the line at any second in case Archer #1 vacates the line unexpectedly due to a temporary equipment or execution issue.

      2. Watch remaining time and wind conditions and provide details as required.

      3. Watch Archer #1's progress and execution and provide support and encouragement as needed.

   c. Archer #3 is watching the target through the scope and spotting Archer #1's arrows verbally after each shot.

7. When Archer #1 vacates the shooting line

   a. Archer #1 crosses behind the 1-meter line as quickly as possible, assumes Position #3 and takes over Spotting for Archer #2

   b. Archer #2 crosses the One Meter Line only after Archer #1 has completely vacated the one meter area, steps onto the shooting line, draws an arrow from his quiver and starts his first shot.

   c. Archer #3 goes to Position #2, performs those duties staying ready and providing support to Archer #2.

8. When Archer #2 vacates the shooting line

   a. Archer #2 crosses behind the 1 meter line as quickly as possible, assumes Position #3 and takes over Spotting for Archer #3

   b. Archer #3 crosses the 1-meter line only after Archer #2 has completely vacated the 1 meter area, steps onto the shooting line, draws an arrow from his quiver and starts his first shot.

   c. Archer #1, if he has an arrow or arrows to complete, goes to position #2, performs those duties staying ready and providing support to Archer #3. If he has completed his arrows he simply rotates to Position #2 and provides support.

   d. *Exception* – If Archer #1 has shot his two arrows but Archer #2 has an arrow or arrows to complete then Archer #1 will remain in Position #3 as the Spotter while Archer #2 returns to Position #2 and prepares to return to the line.

9. When Archer #3 vacates the shooting line, there are two possibilities:

   I. If all archers have completed shooting their arrows now is the time to look through the scope to check where your arrows hit and share information with each other as a debriefing and prepare to go to the target and score the end.

II. If arrows remain to be shot then proceed as follows:

a. If Archer #1 has an arrow or arrows remaining he crosses the 1-meter line only after Archer #3 has completely vacated the 1-meter area, steps onto the shooting line, draws an arrow from his quiver and starts his remaining shot(s).

b. If Archer #1 has shot his two arrows and Archer #2 has an arrow or arrows remaining he crosses the 1-meter line only after Archer #3 has completely vacated the 1-meter area, steps onto the shooting line, draws an arrow from his quiver and starts his remaining shot(s).

c. If Archer #3 has an arrow or arrows remaining he assumes Position #2 and prepares to return to the line while the Spotter (Archer #1 or 2) remains in Position #3

10. When the line is vacated

a. Archer #3 crosses the 1 meter line only after Archer #1 or #2 has completely vacated the one meter area, steps onto the shooting line, draws an arrow from his quiver and starts his remaining shot(s).

b. Once all archers have completed shooting their arrows now is the time to look through the scope to check where your arrows hit and share information with each other as a debriefing and prepare to go to the target and score the end.

And for Compound . . .

I have covered the basics of how to shoot the first end of the team round for recurve archers. They will shoot three more ends to complete the match and then either retire or advance based on their performance. I tell my team to just keep shooting until they either make you sit down or put a medal around your neck.

> *Initially panic can set in. All you have to do is to convince them that one thing that all successful archers have learned to do is to shoot aggressively. Not fast, not rushed, not hurried . . . just aggressively.*

The minor differences I referred to relating to Team Rounds for compound archers are primarily distance, target difference, and the "trickeration" of the rules. Many things in the world of archery make sense to me but the reasoning behind the Compound archers shooting 50 m while the Recurve Archers shoot 70 m just escapes my understanding. However, they at least kept the distance 50 m for Compound Team Round. Also, even though there is room for three team round targets on the mat the rules call for two targets and for teams to shoot three arrows in each!

As a result of this unusual arrangement teams must decide their approach to make this happen. One approach is to have each archer shoot one arrow into each target. Another approach is to assign Archer #1 to the left target, Archer #2 to the right target and Archer #3 to shoot one in each target. Both are acceptable, but I will give you one important piece of advice. Archer #3 needs to be flexible enough to respond to the spotter and shoot the target that needs an arrow. The reason I say that is occasionally even the best plan goes bad and archers have a mental breakdown and shoot the wrong target or are caught by the wind and miss the target they were shooting at but luckily hit the other target. Well Archer #3 needs to be able to pick up the pieces and finish out in a way that the whole team still looks like heroes.

Summary
Just in this brief introduction to the team round you begin to see how interesting it is and how much fun it can be. In another chapter, I will get much deeper into the preparation of a team to give them their best chance to win.

On Coaching Collegiate Archery

The supporting audience for the Mixed Team Round may just be the other members of the team but, still, that's a lot of noise!

14

The Team Round – Part 2 Coaching to Win

Imagine if you will, the U.S. National Outdoor Collegiate Championships (USNOCC) is scheduled for mid to late May and it's time to get your team ready for the greatest show on earth—500 college kids dedicated to the sport of archery all converging on the same field in the same college town to determine:

1. Who the best collegiate archers and collegiate archery teams in the United States are and
2. Just how much fun this many collegiate archers in one spot can have in just one week.

    While a few archers may get confused as to which of these is most important at the beginning of the tournament, but by the end of the Awards Banquet and Party just about all of the archers will have a personal investment in both quests. A great time is had by all. But back to business.

    I always try to get the team to come back to school three or four days before we leave for Nationals for final preparations and training for the Team Rounds which we break into two to three days. This allows me to have them all there at the same time for final teaching points in preparation for what will be the biggest and most important archery tournament many of them will ever shoot in. Most importantly, these few days finally give me a chance to really work on the team round.

How do you select the teams?

What the heck am I talking about here? The way the collegiate team round competition is set up the tournament staff will seed the teams based on the three highest qualifying scores from each school in a competitive discipline and that is who is expected to shoot . . . unless the team representative/coach chooses to provide a roster that overrides these default assignments. This list must be provided to the tournament director at least one hour prior to the start of the team round in question.

You might be thinking: "What fool wouldn't want his top three shooters in the team round?" Well, occasionally I'd be that fool. Most of the time schools have just three archers in a division, or such a gap in performance levels that it is obvious who you want to shoot the team round. However, occasionally some teams and coaches are blessed with better than average depth, and you have more than three archers competing for the three official spots on the team. On those occasions I don't necessarily want to shoot my three best. I want to shoot my best three.

This strategy requires more work and puts you out there in an area where you may, heck, you will, be criticized. Win or lose, somebody's kid sits when they think he should have shot, and if your team doesn't perform as well as you hoped, it is your fault and no one else's. I believe that here is where you do team building. I start by explaining to them that to have the best chance of winning we need the team that works best together and that I will work directly with them to see which combination performs best together and through a 360 degree evaluation of sorts what combination gives the team members the greatest confidence in their potential success. Then, assuming they have bought into this team concept, you and the squad captain will make the final decision.

How do you give your whole team the opportunity to practice the team round?

First, I recommend that you set a starting time for your team round practice that provides your archers plenty of time to work on other things before hand. That resolves the excuses such as "I didn't have time to get my sight setting" or "I didn't have time to warm up."

Make sure you have enough mats and stands up to accommodate all of your archers in groups of three. Put together what you think your natural teams are and let the others form teams even if you have to mix men and women Recurve, Compound, Bowhunter, or Barebow archers into teams for this practice. During this practice, you will simply let everyone practice the timing, the transitions between archers, the spotters' responsibilities, and the deck responsibilities as discussed in the previous chapter. You are just trying to give everyone some general practice at all positions in the Team Round. I would budget a half an hour to an hour for this stage of the training. I try to have them do this several days during spring practice so everyone gets an opportunity to become comfortable with the round.

One position in the Team Round that is highly under rated is that of

Spotter. Teams often lose points and matches if the spotter is either slow or inaccurate in their spot. So come up with a plan. With everything else going on teaching people how to spot is often overlooked. Either use a magnet on a metal backed target patch or use a uniform system of calling. Explain to them that with a budgeted time of only 20 seconds per arrow they have to stay on the scope until the arrow hits and then make an immediate call. Just move the magnet to the correct position on the target patch and hold it up for the archer to see. If not using the target patch then just make a simple call such as: "10 at 3 o'clock," "9 at 6," or "7/8 line at 9." These are simple calls that are easily understood, and if callers instead try to be colorful or entertaining in their calls frustration and misunderstandings that can affect the team's performance and ultimate success can occur. Calls need to be clear and concise.

How do you select your three person team?

Put all your archers on the one meter line and set the clock to 40 seconds. Blow the whistle twice to get them ready, then blow it once to start the time, have them approach the line and shoot their two arrows. If the groups in the target will allow it, you can repeat this as many as two more times before sending them to the target to score. Shoot enough ends of the team round to get a reasonable sampling. We are doing this in an effort to see who scores best with the timing of the team round in effect and eliminate from consideration those who clearly are not ready to contribute in the team round. You can normally accomplish this in about 30 minutes.

Once we have cut the archers in consideration for each team down to four or five, allow them to practice the team round under normal timing while rotating different archers into the mix. You want each team to practice all combinations of personnel keeping a record of the scores of all combinations until you and the squad captain have determined which is the most productive group of three archers on the squad. They should be able to take care of this in less than an hour.

Now that you have your three person team, what will be the order of the line-up?

Ninety percent of the time you will see the top shooter on a team shooting as the #3 archer anchoring the team. In some cases that can be the right decision, however this is where my sadistic side starts to show.

1. **Get an Average** For the next practice we take those three man teams, putting all team members on the one meter line and, using only a whistle and a stopwatch, start the 40 second ends again. We want to collect data on 24 arrows per archer to get an average score per arrow. If your teams can safe-

ly shoot two or even three ends of team round before scoring, without damaging arrows, that will cut down considerably on the on the walk time and change a one hour exercise into 30 minutes.

2. **Introduce Time Constraints** Now blow them to the line and announce a 30 second end. Shoot it, then score it and return to the line. Next do it with 20 seconds. Then follow that with 15 seconds. Then repeat the exercise with 30 seconds again, then 15 seconds again and close out with 20 seconds again. Now tabulate the scores. Your anchor man should be the archer whose score decays the least when the time gets pinched. I only list 6 ends for this exercise because an exercise like this is designed to test not train. While I need to know how they react to these time constraints I understand that many archers will find extended practice with these constraints to be counter-productive to their development. This step should take less than 30 minutes to complete.

3. **Choosing the Order** For example, if your top archer averages 9.5 when he has 40 seconds but only 7 when forced to shoot in 15 seconds, your next archer averages 9 with 40 seconds but 7 with 15 seconds but your third archer averages 7.5 with 40 seconds and 7 with 15 seconds, smart money would put archer number three in the anchor position. Why? Because he has demonstrated that he only loses a half a point when he is forced to shoot under a serious time constraint, while the other shooters lose 2 and $2\frac{1}{2}$ points each under the same constraint.

You've got to believe!

My next strategy is to sell them on their ability to win the event. I do this by sharing the performances that have won in the past and showing them how close their performances have been to these winning performances. Then I leave them with the thought that winning any elimination round is as simple as properly executing a few shots at the right time and the team who does that will be the winner.

Expect the Unexpected!

One last thing my sadistic side likes involves getting them used to stress by imposing crisis during one of their remaining team round practices. Set up for a normal team round practice to be run by a timing clock and a whistle. Now simply start the team round by shooting at least one regular end. On the second or third end start imposing one crisis after another where once they start the end, an archer is going to full draw when you shout "abort" requiring the archer to put down the shot and clear the line for the next shooter. Repeat this until you have disturbed all archers at least once during the practice. This drill gets them thinking and will keep them prepared to shift at anytime during the end while learning to stay focused and shoot within the time limit imposed. They will get to the point that when they step to the line they will fear nothing. And that is what I want.

I'm sure there are as many strategies to shooting the team round as there are coaches who coach the team round. I share these thoughts with you in an effort to give these kids the best experience they can have. And a team's successful performance is about as great an experience as they can have in collegiate archery.

This photo is of Bob with archery immortal Fred Bear and a world record trophy Grizzly Bear that Fred shot. Fred had to tame "the Shakes" to make that shot!

15

Taming the Shakes

"Coach, how can I make myself stop shaking?"

Coaches can help fix a number of things on the spot, but generally speaking, this is not one of them. Well, I have one trick but the best way for a coach to fix problems with shaking, twitching, muscle spasms. and other involuntary muscle movements in his archers is through coaching and teaching prevention.

If we are going to teach our archers how to prevent these involuntary muscle movements we must first breakdown the causes. For the purposes of this chapter we will address only benign involuntary movements and not those which are symptoms of serious illnesses such as Lou Gehrig's disease or muscular dystrophy.

Possible Causes
1. Stress
2. Lack of Sleep
3. New Medication
4. Dehydration
5. Fatigue
6. Nutrient Deficiency
7. Stimulants

I will address each of the possible causes along with how to prevent them from causing or contributing to the involuntary muscle movement.

Stress

We all have stress in our lives. As a coach, you want to help your students every step along the way, but there are limitations. While you can help them with life skills by advising the best way to limit stress from schoolwork such as tests, presentations, and papers due is to stay on top of them. Once you start to get behind anywhere it starts to snowball, eventually leaving you with the fear of impending doom. We need to be more careful when it comes to finances or the minefield that is personal relationships. The best you can ever do there will come best in the form of general guidance, avoiding specifics to the death.

Lack of Sleep

College students are young and resilient. They think they are indestructible and when they drink they're positive that they're bullet proof too. So, they will be very resistant to your suggestions concerning the value of a regular routine of sleep, meaning a consistent time to go to bed and a consistent number of hours of sleep each night. Make the suggestion anyway.

Taking this plan on the road for an archery tournament is even tougher. The first night in the motel the team can be just like the first night of summer camp. Half of the team, excited by being away from home with their friends, tries to pull an all-nighter which ends up leaving everyone sleep deprived. Remind them that getting a good night's sleep the night before a tournament will help them towards their goal to shoot a personal best tomorrow.

New Medications

Obviously, your health is a little beyond coaching but it is important to understand that anytime a doctor prescribes a new medication it may come with undesirable side effects. I recommend to my students to make sure that the new meds: 1) are not on the list of substances banned by the USOC and 2) that they have read the list of side effects to make sure they don't cause involuntary tremors or shakes. If they do, have them ask their doctor to look for a different prescription.

Dehydration

Coaches in all sports are constantly preaching to their students to stay hydrated. While going to the bathroom can be inconvenient during a competition it is important to keep drinking. Not only does it keep your muscles working properly it can keep you alive. When shooting in Baton Rouge at an Olympic Festival many years ago a fellow competitor watched me staggering back from the shooting line and threw a cold wet towel on the back of my neck. When he did it was like someone just change the channel from a black and white station to full color. I was about to pass out and didn't have a clue. Dehydration sneaks up on you and can take a toll. So keep drinking! (If you are urinating, you are not dehydrated . . . normally.)

Fatigue

Every year the new students make the same mistakes. They are trying to develop their bodies as well as their minds by scheduling every exercise class and activity they fit into their itinerary. However, when they come to archery practice and they can't lift their bows or go to full draw without shaking I have to ask them what in the world is going on. They advise me that they just came from the University Recreation Center where they were pumping iron for the last hour. I think my standard response is, "I love you . . . but you're killing me!"

I then request them to do that after practice or on off days from now on and it generally solves the problem. The good news is that it seldom if ever happens on the day of a tournament.

Nutrient Deficiencies

I believe that getting the necessary nutrients to live a healthy life is not my concern with the average college student. What we like to point out here is that anyone who has a problem with involuntary muscle movement, whether it be twitching, flinching, jerking, or shaking there are nutrients that can be helpful in combating this problem. According to the University of Maryland Medical Center a lack of vitamin C, vitamin E or potassium may trigger small involuntary muscle movement such as the ones we are discussing here. The mineral calcium and other vitamins (vitamins D, B-6 and B-12) have been long known to improve muscle efficiency.

Stimulants

The use and especially the overuse of stimulants such as caffeine (in coffee, tea, soft drinks and energy drinks) are known to contribute to shaking and other involuntary muscle movements. Plus archery is one of the few sports that has banned alcohol from competition (WADA dropped its ban but World Archery re-instituted it in 2018). I encourage archers to wean themselves off of caffeine, sugar, and alcohol when they join the team. I've never known those items to contribute to the performance of any athlete. After having this talk with them when we get to our first tournament I'm really confused when I see a kid who makes the decision to skip coffee at breakfast go to the field and chug one Mtn Dew after another until I catch him. I ask him what the heck he's thinking about and he tells me there's no caffeine in soft drinks. Next year I'll use brighter crayons when I draw them a picture about caffeinated drinks.

The easy take away from our look at this topic is that Sleep, Water and Exercise are our friends while Alcohol and Caffeine (in Coffee, Tea, Sodas and Energy Drinks) are the enemy. It is obviously more complicated as we discussed.

The Trick

I would like to turn your attention to those pesky muscles that cause us all the problems.

Our muscles are made of slow-twitch and fast-twitch muscle fibers. The slow-twitch red fibers provide strength and endurance and are the ones that do all the real work for us in archery. These slow-twitch muscle fibers provide your voluntary muscle movement. The fast-twitch white muscle fibers produce small amounts of energy very quickly and as a result are the main culprit in the unwanted involuntary muscle movements we have been discussing in this chapter.

People who struggle to find the time to exercise properly sometimes find themselves fidgeting, bouncing their legs, or just feeling like they have to move. I have discovered that expending the excess energy levels in the fast twitch muscle fibers through exercise the evening before an event helps to minimize the twitching, jerking and shaking we experience as involuntary muscle movements. Always make sure your team gets a sufficient amount of exercise the night before a competition. I always encourage a nice run, working out in the motel's exercise room or swimming a few laps in the pool. However, if you are lacking proper exercise facilities and some of your kids aren't runners I have come up with another option to accomplish our goals. I've been using it personally for over 40 years and refer to it fondly as "Beating Air."

Beating Air

Note Before performing this exercise make sure to have participants warm up their muscles, especially in their upper body.

1. Place a straight back chair in the middle of an open area like the center of a motel room.
2. Sit down on the chair with your feet flat on the floor and your back against the back of the chair.
3. Relax completely with eyes closed and your arms hanging down by your sides.
4. Now take several deep cleansing breaths to relax while you think of your happy place. e.g. Lying in the shade by a beautiful babbling brook.
5. Slowly begin to swing your arms ever so slightly, back and forth.
6. Gradually increase the amount of movement in your arms, swinging them back and forth and starting to slowly open and close your hands.
7. Allow the movement to start to get more violent with the arms going back and forth and crossing themselves in front of your torso while opening and closing your hands.

8. The movement will reach maximum intensity when your buttocks seem to be coming out of the chair. Maintain this intensity until you feel physically tired.

9. Once you feel tired reverse the cycle. Start slowing the movement down a little at a time until you are barely moving and you are starting to relax again.

10. Try to assess how your muscles feel as your arms almost come to a stop. At this point you should feel as if your energy is restored.

11. If you feel like you have the energy to continue you should start the process again. Once you feel spent start the slow down process again.

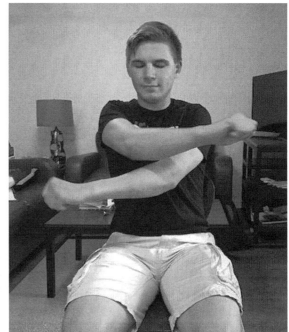

Matt Petty demonstrates Beating Air which is used to provide a brief workout the night before competition when other exercise routines are not available.

12. Normally, two or three cycles is enough to accomplish our goal.

When I use this technique, I am steady as a rock the next day. While not everybody reports shooting better after trying this, I've never heard of anyone who shot worse. It is a very convenient pre-tournament exercise plan to take on the road. So, give it a try the next time you shoot a tournament and let me know how it worked for you and your team.

Bob Ryder

For Just You

Bob Ryder with USA Archery's National Coach Kisik Lee after being certified as a USA Archery Level 4 NTS Coach.

16

Sharpening the Saw

Reign in your ego. It's time for a reality check. You have all heard the old saying by Abraham Maslow:

"If the only tool you have is a hammer, you tend to see every problem as a nail."

In many ways, coaches validate this quote. Every one of us has our own set of experiences in competition, in hunting, in education, in training, and in life in general. Much of our strength as coaches comes from being able to draw from these experiences when we are faced with the challenges that our kids present us. As a coach, when we are approached by one of our kids asking a serious question about something affecting his performance, we never want to say, "Gee kid, . . . I just don't know." Instead we try to reach back into our memory bank and when we find nothing particularly relevant we simply pull out our "hammer" and take a swat at this kid's unusual "nail."

Is that really the best we can do? Sometimes a better choice would be to confide in this archer that he has presented you a with an interesting problem and while you have some thoughts, you don't want to steer him wrong and would like to dig a little bit and get back with him on this issue at your next practice.

How can we reduce the frequency of these delayed responses or possibly even eliminate them? You can do it by . . . Sharpening the Saw. If you don't know the story, the advice given to a young energetic carpenter, who has been sawing away for many minutes and not getting very far is that much less effort is needed if you first "sharpen the saw." This has come down to a recommendation to prepare properly to do a task.

Sharpening your saw as an archery coach can be accomplished in many ways.

1 **Expanding Your Experiential Base** You expand your experiential base every time you shoot another tournament, set up a new bow, make a new

bowstring, or make repairs to equipment that is not functioning properly. As someone who was in his shooting prime 40 years ago, I have had a number of layoffs from competition over the years. This past March I decided to have another go at the U.S. Indoor Championships (first time in 27 years) and found it to be a real Saw Sharpening Event. I was reminded of just how hard it is to do everything I ask kids to do when they are over bowed. When I started to practice I found I was so weak I had to modify my shot process just to shoot some arrows. As I developed strength over the weeks before the competition I was able to get closer to the way I wanted to shoot and ended up only moderately embarrassed at the event. But getting to shoot the event and watch two Olympic Medalists fight it out for number one was great. I had an opportunity to observe the current shot processes of both Vic Wunderle (Silver & Bronze 2000) and Jacob Wukie (Silver 2012). When at an event with top competitors, like these two, take every opportunity to observe what they are doing and how they are doing it. Even though I enjoyed the opportunity to work with Jacob during his four years on the JMU Archery Team I wasn't about to miss an opportunity to see how he had furthered his game since graduation.

2 **Expanding Your Knowledge Base** Whether you are taking an instructor training class or teaching it, you will be expanding your knowledge base. Conscientious instructors always spend some time preparing knowing that that will induce some new thoughts. It never ceases to amaze me the interesting problems and issues that are brought up by the students in a class.

Take every opportunity to be a student or an instructor in classes related to our sport. Types of classes or courses that you can attend that will provide opportunities to increase a knowledge base that is helpful to archery coaches are:

Shooting
Instructing
Coaching
Officiating
Tournament Management
Sports Psychology
Nutrition
Conditioning
Equipment
Arrow Building
Making Bowstrings
Tuning

You have the opportunity to hear from a lot of different people on a lot of different topics. When it comes to people's suggestions, listen to everyone on everything, but accept nothing without testing it out yourself. Naturally there are exceptions, but as a general rule you have a responsibility to be right so a basis for recommending things comes with a little more than casual accountability.

I've been on the U.S. Archery Team and attended their camps. I was on the USAA Board of Governors when we formalized the program which set up the Instructor and Coach's Schools establishing the Coaching Levels for USA Archery. I attended a Level 1 & 2 Instructors School and then a Level 3 Course at the Lake Placid Olympic Training Center. Several years ago I completed a Level 4 Coaches course at the Chula Vista Olympic Training Center.

By attending this program with instructors including KiSik Lee, Jim White, Guy Krueger, John Crawley, Dr. H. Lee, and Steve Cornell I was exposed to the latest version of the National Training System. To be honest with you, I enjoyed getting an opportunity to learn from the perspectives of the other coaches in the class. The combined years of coaching experience in the room out there was very impressive and I was excited to draw from as much of it as possible.

That being said, I would be remiss if I didn't spend some time discussing the most practical method of expanding your knowledge base. The instructional books that have been written, the magazines that have been published, the DVD's that have been produced and the YouTube videos that have been posted provide an unlimited supply of information available at your fingertips "on-demand."

Archery Focus magazine is clearly one of the best sources of reference material in the sport of archery and it is available 24 hours a day, seven days a week. Steve Ruis and Claudia Stevenson do a wonderful job of bringing today's archery topics to life through interesting articles written by active coaches and archers and other experts in related fields. But more valuable even than their bi-monthly magazine is the wealth of information contained in the searchable archives of the back issues of *Archery Focus*. Just this week I was reading an article by Larry Wise in the September issue and then popped back to an issue in 1997 where I found myself enjoying articles written by Rick McKinney, Lisa Franseen and wait for it . . . Larry Wise. I'm sure he must have written it as a child.

If I'm not wanting to sit at the computer sometimes I can sharpen my blade simply by reaching for something good on my own bookshelf. Whether I am seeking a new perspective, searching for reinforcement of my own position on a topic or just looking for a Whack on the Side of the Head

I can make a selection from my own library. Right there on my own bookshelf I have a selection of books providing me good counsel from KiSik Lee, Rick McKinney, Michelle Frangilli, Hyung Tak Kim, Larry Wise, Steve Ruis, Simon Needham, Lanny Basham, and Terry Wunderle to mention just a few.

These guys help keep me surrounded with good information at my fingertips at all times. I have also enjoyed having DVD's from Larry Wise, KiSik Lee, Dave Cousins, and others when I want to share visually with groups I work with. It's amazing how helpful it is to share words of wisdom from the horse's mouth when trying get the attention a topic deserves. By starting and stopping the DVD at strategic points you are actually able to drive home points more effectively whether in support of the content or not.

3   **Revving Up Your Engine** YouTube has become the center of the universe for many individuals seeking instruction on archery. While much of the instruction on YouTube does not serve as inspiration to me, the broad appeal of this medium is very inspiring. Just type "YouTube Archery Instruction" into your web browser and see just how many things have been posted. While much of this instruction is not terribly inspiring, the part of the archery presence on YouTube that does get me excited is World Archery TV. All I have to do is type in "World Archery TV," then select instruction, or one of the many head to head medal matches from World Cup, World Championship or Olympic Games competitions and I am set. I instantly become an Internet junky until I have to go someplace or something jumps out at me that I just have to do after watching action or instruction that I have chosen. Sometimes it inspires me to present something differently when I am coaching or try something different when I am shooting. But either way, it has an influence on me, gives me a whack on the side of the head, and helps "Sharpen My Saw."

The shooting field of the 2015 U.S. National Outdoor Collegiate Championships hosted by JMU. Starting small is recommended but eventually programs may want to step up to the plate for these major events.

17

Hosting Your Own Tournament

Each of us in the sport of archery has to follow our own path. Whether you are currently an archer, a coach, an official, or a tournament director you probably started as simply an archer. What is important is to keep your eyes open and constantly evaluate the needs of your team and our sport and contribute in a manner that provides an opportunity to strengthen your team and grow our sport.

If you are currently coaching a college archery team then you have probably discovered that your team's competitive opportunities are limited by the financial support that the team enjoys. Since the beginning of time, one thing that has remained a constant is that "Necessity is the Mother of Invention." Depending on the administrative guidelines your team has to follow you may or may not be able to improve your revenue picture. However, one way that you can expand your team's competitive experience while controlling your expenses is to host tournaments.

While it is possible for some schools to actually use a tournament to raise money for their team I want suggest to you that not all tournaments are a source of revenue. On my list of why you should run an archery tournament at your school, to make money would be closer to the bottom of the list than the top.

My number one reason for wanting to run archery tournaments at JMU is to provide an event that serves as a positive quality competitive experience for my team and other competitors who choose to participate. Second is my desire to reduce the travel costs and academic strain for the team during the season. Hosting tournaments also serves the team by increasing their visibility and establishing their school as a recognized hub of activity for the sport of archery in the area. This makes it easier to hold successful shooting clinics and coaching seminars when the time comes.

I'm going to assume that if you're still reading this that you are at least open to the thought of hosting a tournament at your school. I'm not sure that those who stopped reading when I suggested hosting your own tournament don't enjoy better mental health than the rest of us but I'm glad some of you are just nuts enough to consider going out on a limb with me one more time.

It's time for another confession. While I have run over 50 National Championships, including U.S. Indoors, National Outdoor Target Championships, National Field Championships, World Team Trials, and Olympic Festivals, I am not going represent what follows in this chapter as a guide to run such involved events. Instead, I will try to provide you a simple summary to getting started in hosting tournaments with a focus on planning and will provide additional information in future offerings to provide the guidance necessary to prepare you to run whatever event you choose.

What Do You Need to Run an Archery Tournament?
Good Question! The answer . . .

#1 – Staff

#2 – Equipment

The staffing required varies with each tournament and while the specific tasks that tournament staff are responsible for is fairly consistent from one event to another the size of the event will have the greatest influence on the staffing that is required. While I have run events with as many as 85 volunteers and 20 paid staff I still have fond memories of running tournaments when I was the only volunteer.

Of all the tasks that you and your staff have to perform the #1 task would have to be planning for the event

Planning
Here's a listing of the elements of any event plan.

A. **Schedule the Event** While it is impossible for all tournaments to be held without conflict it is important when planning a new event that you make every effort to avoid traditional dates of established local, regional, and national events. If you are bidding to host a rotating event the date should already be established and your bid will just be to establish the host and location. If you are bidding to host a major event you may be preparing a written proposal for an event that can be as much as two years down the road.

B. **Book the Facility** Book facilities as early as possible. Do not assume that the venue you want to use is available without first checking with the powers that be. If your tournament involves more than just a shooting field make sure you book all facilities you hope to use well in advance. Just this year, I was awarded the U.S. National Collegiate Outdoor Championship

Staff is the most important component of your success when running a tournament. Andy Puckett has been my right hand man in all the tournaments we have run since the mid 90's. He's the best and not for sale. Photo Courtesy of Teresa Crawford

one year earlier than what my bid was for. With 6 months notice I was fortunate to be able to book the athletic field I wanted for the event and an entire park for our cookout but due to the short lead time (need 18 months) I was unable to book the facility I had planned on for the Awards Banquet and had to settle for a sub-par venue for the event.

C. **Register the Event** Whether you are just registering a sanctioned event or applying for a Star FITA make sure you get this done. There is nothing worse than a guy shooting a new world record and not having it recognized because somebody forgot to apply for a Star.

D. **Design the Field Layout** It is important to review World Archery rules when planning the layout of your field. In addition to providing all of the recommended lines and safety barriers, your field needs to be oriented so that archers are shooting north.

E. **Seek Local Support** By approaching the local Chamber of Commerce and letting them know what you are planning, some businesses may come forward with offers of free or discounted supplies that you need for the event. Local motels will offer discounted rooms or comp rooms for your staff. Restaurants will often offer discount coupons to competitors or free meals to coaches and officials.

F. **Seek Sponsors** There are no limits to where you can search for sponsors. While the archery industry in inundated with requests to support events, it never hurts to ask. Other good potential sponsors are the bigger local shops and manufacturers of related products such as optics. Try mailing your request for sponsorships three to six months ahead of the event, follow with an email two weeks after the mailing and follow the email with a phone call within a week of the email.

G. **Print a Tournament Program** So much of our communication prior to and during events is done electronically on event web sites or through email we often forget about that cash cow that is the Tournament Program. If you make a concerted effort to sell ads in the program while you are seeking the local support and sponsors many businesses will buy an ad as an inexpensive way of supporting the event and they can justify that support out of their advertising budget. Also include an opportunity on your website and in registration confirmation for anybody to purchase spots for special messages and good luck banners in the program. Remember every little bit helps.

H. **Schedule Special Activities** Whether it's a cook-out, a party, a banquet, or a special seminar you can make your tournament a special event with a little extra planning. Sometimes you can get companies to underwrite the cost of one of these events just for the opportunity of getting sponsor recognition and putting up a banner at the event.

I **Line Up your DOS and Officials** While in National Events the Director of Shooting (DOS) and the officials are appointed by the Officials and Rules Committee of USA Archery local and regional events are not. You will need to contact a someone to serve as your DOS and you will need to arrange officials based on the number of targets. The general rule is to have one official for every ten targets on the field.

Use these planning topics as a guide to get started putting together your first event. Don't hesitate to contact me with any questions or suggestions you have.

Equipment – Recurve

Is there anything prettier than a new bow? This is my most recent recurve setup.

18

Equipment Selection for New Recurve Archers

You may have been hired as the Coach of a collegiate archery team and as such you may have assumed that you were taking over a team of experienced and well-equipped archers. I think it's time for your wake-up call.

As the coach of a collegiate archery team you will be expected to coach the archers who make up your team. If you hope to keep your job as coach you will want to recruit experienced archers for your team. If you hope to field a full team you will want to develop the talent that you aren't fortunate enough to recruit. If you want the new kids to compete they will need to have suitable equipment. If you want your team to be competitive you will need to teach them basic skills, recommend basic equipment for them, set-up the new equipment, coach them and do the final tuning of their equipment. Oops, I failed to mention that you'll probably dabble in strength and conditioning and developing their mental game.

Sorry about the scare tactics. All I was really trying to do is to let you know that you may be spending a fair amount of time working on the equipment side of the game. For new archers, this is not that difficult.

Recommending Recurve Equipment

Once you've recruited new archers, introduced them to the basic skills, and let them shoot your equipment or the schools equipment long enough to get them to ask about buying their own, it's time to pop the big question? "What's your budget?" This is a hugely important question that should be asked before you start talking about any specific equipment because regardless the price range you want to have presented the options in a way that they will have full confidence in the equipment they buy. If you start describing a $2,500 set up and they have a $500 budget for everything you will then have to explain the things they are losing with every dollar they take away from the package. I'd

115

rather have you tout the value of the items that they can afford. I can't turn anyone away though, so even if they don't have any money, if they are interested and appear dedicated I will try to find loaner equipment until they find themselves in a position to be able to buy their own.

That being said, when it comes to archery equipment, even more so than with things in general, buy the best you can afford. It's like I said when I was representing Zeiss Binoculars and Scopes, "I'd rather explain the features that justify the price once to a customer than to apologize to him the rest of my life for the poor quality."

I always encourage my archers to develop a relationship with a local pro shop who can provide them guidance in all things equipment. If they don't have a local pro shop that specializes in recurve target archery or they don't trust what they are hearing then I am more than happy to provide the guidance they need.

Recommending a Bow

We always recommend to our new archers that they purchase ILF (International Limb Fitting) Risers and Limbs to provide maximum flexibility in the purchase of different brands of limbs, the switching out of limbs to change weight as the need arises, and the ability to resell the equipment if the archer wants to make a change.

The Riser They can save money easily here. Low-end to mid-range risers perform consistently and lack mainly in fit and finish over higher-end risers.

The Limbs Their first set of limbs will definitely not be their last. For shooting indoors they can save tons of money on that first set of limbs by buying low end wood laminated limbs. If they're buying them to shoot outdoors they can save money by getting low-end to mid-range carbon laminated limbs. Once they get near what you think will be their final weight limbs, they should go for broke and get the best they can afford. The extra performance and stability can help to put them over the top.

Right- or Left-Handed?

Since you hope to be working with this new archer for an extended period of time, maybe even four years, they should choose their bow based on your eye dominance test. Notice, I said your eye dominance test. Don't take the archer's word for what their eye dominance is and don't just let anyone do the test. Take the time to check it yourself so you know it's right.

Group Testing of Eye Dominance Have your archers stand facing you approximately ten feet away, with the fingers on both hands fully extended and both arms fully extended toward you have them overlap both thumbs forming a small triangle. Have them look through the small triangle with both eyes open centering your head in the triangle. Next have them pull the triangle back to their faces, keeping your head centered in the triangle until they touch their nose. Have them hold that position until you record which of their eyes you see through their triangles. The eye you see through the triangle is their dominant eye.

Yes, there may be other physical considerations that can make the dominant eye secondary in the choice of bow hand. But please evaluate everything yourself and help the student with their decision. It is perfectly acceptable to have archers shoot right- or left-handed by their choice in a brief camp or initial experience, but I would recommend to individuals making a long-term decision that they elevate eye dominance over hand dominance.

What Length of Bow?

Bow Length Based Upon Draw Length

Draw	Bow	Riser	Limbs
Up to 23″	64″ Bow	23″ Riser	Short Limbs
24″-27″	66″ Bow	23″ Riser	Medium Limbs
28″-30″	68″ Bow	25″ Riser	Medium Limbs
31″	+70″ Bow	27″ w/Med or 25″ w/Long Limbs	

Note I'm from a generation where we like to work the limbs for maximum speed/efficiency. If you want a smoother draw with less finger pinch try adding 2″ to your selection by either bumping the Riser or Limb Length up one size / 2″.

What Weight of Limbs?

Base your recommendation on both their current strength *and* their anticipated development.

I recommend the team stockpile several sets of ILF limbs of different lengths and weights which will take some of the pressure off this decision. I consider the archer's current strength and project the weight they will be able to handle by outdoor season and order that set of limbs. We will then let the archer use a lighter set of limbs as their strength develops in the spring. Their limbs will sit in storage until they are ready for that transition. The last thing you want is an archer who is over bowed or trying to shoot a weight before they are ready.

What Accessories?

To set a bow up they will need more than a riser and a set of limbs. The accessories they will need to complete the set up process and have your new archer ready to shoot include:

1. *Bowstring* Start off new archers on a Fast Flight String because it is relatively inexpensive, yet it performs well and is very reliable.
2. *Arrow Rest* Sometimes less is more. The fewer moving parts and set screws you have on your rest the better. I lean towards simple flipper rests here, but if they can spend a little more, my favorite is the Shibuya Ultima Rest.
3. *Cushion Plunger* This is a simple device where the cheap versions sometimes work as well as the expensive versions. When you go up in price it is mainly for better adjustability and reliability over the long run. If they need to save money on the original purchase buy what their budget requires. They will eventually buy a better one when they can afford it.
4. *Clicker* The simple blade type that attach directly to the riser is relatively inexpensive and should serve well. They may want to splurge and buy a black blade just to cut down the shine.
5. *Bow Sight* This is the one place where I encourage them to invest in the best they can afford. There is a lot going on with a sight and while they can shoot a good score with a cheap sight they will eventually lose their mind trying to keep all the screws tight and fixing their sight because it vibrates into a new location. Basically, the sight manufacturers will say that you can pay me now or pay me later but you will eventually have to get a good sight. I can recommend Axcel or Shibuya.
6. *Stabilizer* This is another area where, while you will want the best when you can afford it, you can find some real savings in buying one of the low-end to mid-range options.

Recommending Arrows

Since we start our new kids off indoors when they buy their equipment we give them the option of buying indoor arrows to get started and buy their outdoor arrows later as we get closer the outdoor season or buying their outdoor arrows right off the bat to shoot year-round.

1. *Indoor* One of the easiest and most reasonable options is still aluminum shafts for indoors. We recommend everything from Tributes to X-7's to our recurve shooters depending on their budgets. I continue to watch for good indoor options from the many all carbon arrows that are targeting that market now. Currently we find that PS-23's and XBusters are good choices for all-carbon indoor arrows.
2. *Outdoor* Obviously, I'd like to have all my kids shooting X10's outdoors but budgets force most into ACG's or ACC's. The reason I like to have my kids shoot these arrows over the excellent all-carbon choices is because we have a reasonably good chance of finding these arrows with a metal detector should they somehow miss the target.

Recommending Finger Tabs

Make sure that the tab you recommend comes with the accessories that your archers may need. While most of the top end tabs include ledges and finger spacers the Cartel *Smart Tab* also comes with these features and a Cordovan leather face at an entry level price.

Recommending Other Accessories

They will need many other accessories that are much less critical to their success where not much guidance is required. Below you will find a list of equipment recommended for all Recurve archers including equipment that is required to be able to shoot and other items that are optional (marked "Optional").

Recommended Equipment List for Recurve Target Archers

Bow
- Riser
- Limbs
- Sight
- Aperture
- Arrow Rest
- Cushion Plunger
- Clicker
- Stabilizer w/weights
- V-bar (Optional)
- V-Bar Rods w/weights (Optional)

String
- Bowstring
- Kisser Button (Optional)

Personal Protection
- Tab
- Armguard
- Bow Sling (Finger or Wrist Sling)
- Chest Protector (Optional)

Arrows (Indoor)
- Shafts (Aluminum/Carbon/Aluminum-Carbon)
- Points
- Nocks
- Fletches (Feathers or Vanes)

Arrows (Outdoor)
- Shafts (Aluminum-Carbon or Carbon)

Points
Nocks
Fletches (Vanes/SpinWings)
Miscellaneous
Quiver
Arrow Puller (Optional)
Arrow Lube (Optional)
Bow Stringer
Bow Stand (Optional)
Bow Case (Soft/Backpack/Hard)
Optics – Binoculars and/or Scope & Tripod (Optional)
Rain Gear (Optional)
Waterproof Shoes/Boots (Optional)
Bow Square (Optional)
Allen Wrenches (Optional)
Bow String Wax (Optional)
Dental Floss (Optional)

These are but a few brief notes to help you provide some guidance to your kids. All we can ever do is do is the best we can to help them in their journey.

One of the myriad details of recurve set up is that the arrow must be centered on the plunger button; here I am making an adjustment to the Shibuya Ultima arrow rest.

19

Basic Set Up for a New Recurve Bow

I feel like it is important to mention that when we initially set a bow up we are setting it up with adjustments designed to perform well for the average user. This will allow the archer to benefit from a properly set up bow while developing his or her skills and specific style. Once the novice has become more consistent as demonstrated by shooting consistent groups we will be able to help him tune the bow and later even teach him to tune the bow.

Steps of Setting up the Recurve Bow

1. *Identify* the top and bottom limbs.
2. *Snap* the top limb into the upper ILF receiver in the riser.
3. *Snap* the bottom limb into the lower ILF receiver in the riser.
4. *Slip* the larger string loop over the top limb sliding it several inches below the string grooves in the top limb.
5. *Install* the smaller string loop into the string grooves in the bottom limb. (Inspect the limb tip grooves for sharp edges before this initial stringing. Sand or file down any sharp spots you find.)
6. *Use a bow stringer to string the bow* sliding the larger loop into the string grooves in the top limb and checking that both string loops are set securely in the string grooves before relaxing the tension on the bow stringer.
7. *Check the brace height* by setting the wide end of the bow square in the pivot point of the grip and measuring the distance to the string at its closest point. Check your measurement against the manufacturer's recommended settings. For this example, we measure a brace height of $8\frac{1}{4}''$ and the manufacturer's recommended setting is $8\frac{1}{4}''$ to $9\frac{1}{4}''$. Since you are at the bottom of the range (making the bow faster but less forgiving) you decide to adjust it to the middle of the range, ($8\frac{3}{4}''$) to start.
8. *Change the brace height* by unstringing the bow, taking the small loop off

the bottom limb, check the direction the string was initially twisted and adding 10 twists to the string in the same direction. Restring and check the brace height again repeating these steps until you reach the desired brace height.

9. *Install the cushion plunger* into the plunger hole directly above the pivot point of the riser (deepest part of the grip) with the body of the plunger initially protruding slightly through the hole into the sight window. Assuming that your young archer will be set up with relatively stiff arrows to start out, set the tension of the button to medium soft to compensate. We will complete installation of the plunger later.

10. *Install the arrow rest* over the plunger body level with the shelf located so the arm of the rest will hold an arrow level with the center of the plunger button.

11. *Install the clicker* by screwing its mounting screw into the clicker hole tapped into the sight window of the riser and tentatively set the blade even with the front edge of the riser.

12. *Snap* the arrow to be shot with this bow on the center serving and set it on the rest under the clicker so that the arrow is approximately level. Make necessary adjustments to the arm of the arrow rest to allow the arrow to be in the center of the button when sitting on the rest.

13. *Install a nocking point locator* approximately $1/4''$ above level using your bow square. Archers who will be shooting small diameter arrows with Easton G-nocks or pin nocks should start out at $3/16''$ and those shooting large diameter shafts with Easton Super Nocks (or the equivalents) should start out at $5/16''$. While I recommend the use of tied on nocking point locators, clamp on brass nocking point locators are just fine for initial set up.

14. *Check the initial draw weight* by
    a. Having the student pull the bow to see if it is a manageable weight.
    or if you have a target weight already in mind
    b. Snap a draw length arrow onto the bowstring and draw with a bow scale to the correct arrow length and then let the bow down and read the recorded weight.

15. *Set the bow to your desired draw weight* by adjusting the limb bolts with an Allen wrench. While there are some variations between manufacturers, I will provide directions for the majority. For this example, we will assume we need to reduce the draw weight four pounds (4 #).
    a. First, unstring your bow to allow easier adjustment and reduce the wear on the threaded components
    b. Next, using an Allen wrench, loosen the set screws on the face of the riser opposite the limb bolts.

c. Now, use the Allen wrench to take two turns off each of your limb bolts rotating the limb bolts counterclockwise.

d. Restring your bow and check the draw weight again. If you reduced the weight three of the 4# try backing another $^2/_3$ to $^3/_4$ of a turn off each bolt and check again. Keep making adjustments until you reach your desired weight.

e. Normally, we would now tighten the set screws but in the initial set up we will move right on to checking the tiller.

16. *Check your tiller* by using your bow square to measure the distance from the base of the top limb, where it attaches to the riser, to the string at its closest position. Then measure the distance from the base of the bottom limb, where it attaches to the riser, and to the string at its closest point. Subtract the measurement recorded for the lower limb from the measurement recorded for the upper limb to get your tiller measurement as it is most commonly referred to, i.e. + $^1/_8$″. The most commonly acceptable range for tiller is from + $^1/_8$″ to + $^1/_4$″. While there are a lot of interesting conversations about recurve tillers outside of that range I think back to something that Earl Hoyt once told

Be sure to check/set the tiller during your initial set-up of a new recurve bow. Photo Courtesy of Andy Puckett

me. He said that, "The specific tiller measurement is not that important . . . just use that tiller measurement to set your nocking point." If your tiller is + $^1/_8$″ then set your nocking point so your arrow is nocked $^1/_8$″ above level. We are trying to optimize the efficiency of our equipment so obviously, we don't want our tiller or nocking point 1″ high or 1″ low.

17. *Set your tiller* using your Allen Wrench. For this exercise, I will assume we want to shoot a + $^1/_8$″ Tiller but our initial measurement is + $^3/_8$″ and that you want to maintain the weight the bow is set at.

a. First, loosen the set screws on the face of the riser opposite the limb bolts.

b. Next, add $^1/_2$ turn onto the top limb bolt while taking $^1/_2$ turn off the bottom limb bolt.

c. Check the tiller again. Repeat process until the tiller is at your desired measurement.

18. *Screw your front stabilizer rod into the stabilizer mounting hole* located just below the grip. There are many options of stabilizer lengths and configurations available but we assume for this example that we have chosen a 30″ front rod for our 68″ bow to keep it both simple and economical for our new archer.

19. *Set your centershot.*

   a. Snap the arrow to be shot on the string under the nocking point and place it on the rest under the clicker blade.

   b. Now set your bow on the ground with the bottom bow tip and the end of the stabilizer touching the ground, propping the bow up with an arrow set in such an angle to have the bow in its most upright position.

   c. Standing behind the bow, position yourself to sight across the string, lining it up with the center of both limbs.
      Note If your limbs are out of alignment (not centered with the riser and string) and your bow features an adjustable limb pocket now is the time to put the limbs in alignment. Since there are several alignment systems employed by different manufacturers please follow the instructions provided by the manufacturer in making the required adjustment.

   d. While in that position sight down the arrow taking note of the relationship between the arrow and the string. You want the string to be in line with the arrow such that the end of the arrow and the entire point shows to the outside of the string, away from the cushion plunger.

   e. Adjusting the centershot. If the arrow's position requires adjustment loosen the set screw in the collar of the cushion plunger. If the arrow show too far outside that alignment you should screw the body of the cushion plunger counterclockwise in its collar to correct the position. If it is too far inside that alignment you should screw the body of the plunger clockwise in its collar. Continue making these adjustments until you have achieved the desired position and then tighten the set screw on the collar.

20. *Install the sight* onto the bow. There are many variations of sights I will simply make a couple of suggestions.

   a. Install your sight mounting block with the manufacturer supplied screws. Since these screws like to vibrate loose save yourself some trouble by using a drop of Loctite *Thread Locker (Blue)* on each of the mounting screws for a little piece of mind. While they will never vibrate loose, they can easily be removed with an Allen wrench.

   b. After completing the assembly of the sight lean the bow up on an arrow again, get in position to look down the string and arrow again, and set the sight's aperture just to the outside of the center of the arrow as it sets on the rest. While you may not be able to set the sight for your new archer this should give him a good starting point left and right.

21. *Install the kisser button*. (This is a good training tool for new archers.)

   a. Have your archer draw the bow to his/her anchor several times until you are satisfied they are going to the anchor you recommend.

   b. Mark the location for the kisser button with a small piece of tape.

   c. Install the kisser button by

      i. *Traditional Kisser Button* Press the button against the string until it pops on. If it is too tight you can slide it onto a small screwdriver first to expand the slot and then slide it off the screwdriver onto the string in the desired location. Then lock it in place by tying it in with dental floss or serving material.

      ii. *Soft Rubber Kisser Button* Unstring your bow, attach a cotter pin like installation tool on the upper string loop, slide the kisser button over the installation tool and down the string to the desired location. Restring your bow. Then lock it in place by tying it in with dental floss or serving material.

The bow is now ready to be shot once the arrows have been cut to work with the clicker. Once your archer is shooting groups consistently you'll be ready to tune it for better performance.

Tuning is a lot easier with high quality components. This is the Beiter cushion plunger, the Rolls-Royce of cushion plangers. Set up and adjustment of these pungers is easy because they also provide all of the tools when you buy the plunger. Many college students, however, may not have the budget to include such pieces, so you will be fiddling with less accommodating accessories.

20

Basic Tuning for Recurves

Life is Good. After weeks of work you look around the room and see that you have several archers grouping well enough for you to take a shot at helping them tune their bows. You can be proud that the instruction and guidance you have given them has brought them this far already. So, let's help them out now by making the set up they are shooting a little more forgiving.

Before we start tuning let's review the major steps we did to set them up originally.

Basic Recurve Bow Set-Up

1. Set Tiller – $1/8''$ Positive
2. Set Nocking Point – $1/4''$ Above Level (Actually from $3/16''$ for small diameter shafts w/Easton G or pin Nocks to $5/16''$ for large diameter shafts w/Easton Super Nocks (or equivalents)
3. Set Centershot – Point Just Outside of Center when viewed from behind

Bare Shaft Tuning

We should spend a few minutes preparing before we start the tuning process. We are going to select the four arrows that your archers are going to shoot in the tuning process.

1. *Check the Components* Make sure all the arrows have the same nocks, fletches and points and that the all components are properly and securely attached. Remove all arrows that do not pass this test from the archer's quiver before tuning.
2. *Check for Straightness* Have them spin their arrows and pick the 4-6 arrows that spin best for them. If they can't spin their arrows to check for straightness you do it for them. Again, remove all arrows that don't pass the spin test before tuning.
3. *Check the Indexing of the Nocks* Make sure that the nocks on all their arrows are turned to the position which should provide the greatest vane clearance for their set up. Any arrow suffering a hard strike on the way past

129

the rest or button will not provide the results you are hoping for.

4. *Check the Nock Fit* Arrows with a nock that is too tight will prevent you from successfully tuning your archers bow. The nock should snap onto the string but the throat size of the nock should be large enough to allow movement on the serving. Proper nock fit should allow the arrow to hang on the string but easily release from the string when you tap the string with two fingers. Any tighter will distort tuning results and any looser will result in inconsistency. If the nock is too tight you can try switching from a small groove nock (.088″) to a large groove nock (.098″), reserve the bowstring with a smaller diameter serving material or switch to a string with fewer strands or simply a smaller diameter string. If the nock is too loose temporarily build up the serving under the nocking point with dental floss. If this works satisfactorily then you can reserve the string with a larger diameter serving material.

5. *Check the Weight* Next, if you have a grain scale, check to see that the arrows match closely in weight. Try to make sure that the four arrows you choose to tune with are within two grains of each other. While two grains will not affect the grouping at any reasonable distance, we are tuning and want as much consistency in the process as possible. When building modern target arrows, we can often keep a set within ± 0.1 grain or so with a reasonable amount of effort. But experience is the real reason I get the grain scale out. On more than one occasion I found that the difficulties I was experiencing tuning for my kids was because some of the arrows were built with regular nibbs while several arrows had weighted points. (NIBB points with 30 grains of lead solder installed). It happened purely by accident through the recycling of old arrows but a lesson was learned none the less.

6. *Make a Bare Shaft* Trim the fletchings off one of the four finalists.

Well now, they said they could shoot groups, so now is the time.

1. Have your archers who are ready to tune warm up their muscles and shoot a few arrows to get ready.

2. Since you are going to have them shoot a bare shaft for the first time it's okay to start them out by having each of them shoot a group at 10 yards with the three fletched arrows selected above. Repeat if necessary to shoot a good group.

3. Have them shoot the bare shaft at the same target. If this shot was a poor shot (bad release, etc) have the archer shoot the bare shaft again.

4. If the bare shaft strikes in the group or within a couple of inches of the group, go ahead and back up to 18 m/20 yds and repeat the exercise before proceeding to step #5. If the bare shaft is more than two inches out of the

group at ten yards move on to step #5.

5. Analyze the results. Once you and your archers agree they have shots in a manner representative of their current skill level it is time to analyze the results. See illustration below:

The Analysis of the Bare Shaft Test Results

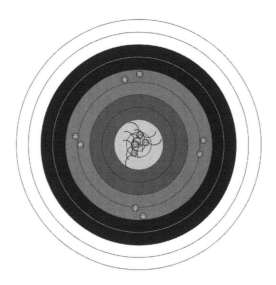

Bare shafts may land left, right, above or below the fletched shaft group . . . or some combination of these.

The analysis of the results is based on the location of the bare shaft as it relates to the group of fletched arrows. I make it a rule to work on the high and low before the left and right due to the fact that every time I ever worked on the left and right first I had to tweak it again after I worked on the high and low.

BS High

If the bare shaft hits above the group of fletched arrows it indicates the bow's nocking point is too low.

Resolution Raise the nocking point.

Move the nocking point up about $\frac{1}{16}''$ and shoot the four arrows again. Continue this process until the bare shaft is impacting the target at the same height as the group of fletched arrows.

Note The reason I suggest you reshoot the fletched arrows and not only the bare shaft is the fact that with every change you make you are chasing the group of fletched arrows with the bare shaft. In other words, every change not only affects the bare shaft but the group location of the fletched shafts as well. The difference is that the bare shaft will move more dramatically and will eventually catch up to the fletched shafts.

BS Low

If the bare shaft hits below the group of fletched arrows it indicates the bow's nocking point is too high.

Resolution Lower the nocking point.

Move the nocking point down about $\frac{1}{16}''$ and shoot the four arrows again. Continue this process until the bare shaft is impacting the target at the same height as the group of fletched arrows.

For Right-Handed Archers

BS Left

If the bare shaft hits to the left of the group of fletched arrows it indicates that the arrow spine is too stiff for the set up.

Resolutions In order of easiest to most drastic.

a. Decrease the spring tension in the cushion plunger $\frac{1}{4}$ turn and try again. Repeat the process until the bare shaft groups with the fletched arrows.

b. Increase the bow poundage by putting one turn on each of the limb bolts and try again. Repeat the process until the bare shaft groups with the fletched arrows.

c. Increase the weight of the points by 10 grains and try again. Repeat this process until the bare shaft groups with the fletched arrows.

d. Reduce the mass weight of the bow by removing some of the stabilizer weights and try again.

e. Change to arrows of weaker spine and try again.

f. Change to longer arrows of the same spine and try again.

BS Right

If the bare shaft hits to the right of the group of fletched arrows it indicates that the arrow spine is too weak for the set up.

Resolutions In order of easiest to most drastic.

a. Increase the spring tension in the cushion plunger $\frac{1}{4}$ turn and try again. Repeat the process until the bare shaft groups with the fletched arrows.

b. Decrease the bow poundage by taking one turn off each of the limb bolts and try again. Repeat the process until the bare shaft groups with the fletched arrows.

c. Decrease the weight of the points by 10 grains and try again. Repeat this process until the bare shaft groups with the fletched arrows.

   d. Cut ¼″ off the length of the arrows and try again. Repeat this process until the bare shaft groups with the fletched arrows or the arrows would no longer be long enough for your archer.

   e. Increase the mass weight of the bow by adding stabilizer weights and try again.

   f. Change to arrows of stiffer spine and try again.

For Left-Handed Archers

BS Left

If the bare shaft hits to the left of the group of fletched arrows it indicates that the arrow spine is too weak for the set up.

Resolutions In order of easiest to most drastic.

   a. Increase the spring tension in the cushion plunger ¼ turn and try again. Repeat the process until the bare shaft groups with the fletched arrows.

   b. Decrease the bow poundage by taking one turn off each of the limb bolts and try again. Repeat the process until the bare shaft groups with the fletched arrows.

   c. Decrease the weight of the points by 10 grains and try again. Repeat this process until the bare shaft groups with the fletched arrows.

   d. Cut ¼″ off the length of the arrows and try again. Repeat this process until the bare shaft groups with the fletched arrows or the arrows would no longer be long enough for your archer.

   e. Increase the mass weight of the bow by adding stabilizer weights and try again.

   f. Change to arrows of stiffer spine and try again.

BS Right

If the bare shaft hits to the right of the group of fletched arrows it indicates that the arrow spine is too stiff for the set up.

Resolutions In order of easiest to most drastic.

   a. Decrease the spring tension in the cushion plunger ¼ turn and try again. Repeat the process until the bare shaft groups with the fletched arrows.

   b. Increase the bow poundage by putting one turn on each of the limb bolts and try again. Repeat the process until the bare shaft groups with the fletched arrows.

   c. Increase the weight of the points by 10 grains and try again.

Repeat this process until the bare shaft groups with the fletched arrows.

d. Reduce the mass weight of the bow by removing some of the stabilizer weights and try again.

e. Change to longer arrows of the same spine and try again.

f. Change to arrows of weaker spine and try again.

Once you have helped them complete the tuning process make sure they go back and build enough additional arrows to match the four used in the tuning process.

I like the bare shaft tuning method. It makes sense that if you can shoot an unguided missile consistently in the same group as your fletched arrows it will be a relatively forgiving set-up.

While bare shaft tuning satisfies the needs of most recurve archers, there are more advanced tuning techniques which I share with you in coming chapters that should give your kids even more forgiveness in their set ups. This may be just what you need to put your archers over the top.

Being able to demonstrate what you are talking about goes a long way with college kids.

21

More Tuning for Recurves

We need to always continue the search for an edge for our archers over their competitors by perfecting their shot or fine tuning for greater forgiveness in their set up. We're not going to get into building of arrows, at this point, but one thing you might want to consider, like we did when we chose our arrows to tune with indoors, is to make sure the arrows they are trying to tune are straight and are matched as closely in weight as possible. One more thing we can do in that endeavor is to try some fine tuning. While it is always a good idea to have all your arrows numbered for tracking purposes, make sure before beginning any fine tuning that all of your archers have numbered their arrows and have a notebook to record specific observations.

As we move forward in our efforts to fine tune our equipment let's remember one simple rule.

"We don't tune for pretty . . . we tune for group!"

While we will often watch the arrows fly or come out of the bow to make certain determinations, the bottom line is your score and that all comes from how your arrows group. Thank goodness, when we get that final tune that produces your best groups the arrow flight you can observe will be what you were hoping for in the first place.

Fine Tuning for Indoor Competition

After successfully helping your students with bare shaft tuning at 18 m their arrows should be flying and grouping pretty well. One thing that you can help them do to improve the forgiveness of their set ups is it to spend a little time perfecting both their nocking point location and plunger tension. I recommend a little tuning exercise I like to call "Taggin' the Line."

137

Taggin' the Line

Have each of your archers who are shooting consistently enough to benefit from some fine tuning take electrical tape or painter's tape wide enough that they can easily see it at 18 m and put it in a straight line across the back side a target face or on a piece of cardboard.

Focusing on the Nocking Point

1. Have your archers hang their targets up with the line running horizontal.
2. Have your archers to shoot six arrows across the line while concentrating on keeping their sight pins on the tape. We don't care about left and right spacing, only our elevation and staying on the line.
3. Pull any bad shots out of consideration and then measure the group variance/height in height; record the variance.
4. Have them adjust their nocking points up $1/16''$ and then repeat the exercise recording the change and the variance for each new location. If the variance decreases continue moving the nocking point up in $1/16''$ increments until the variance increases.
5. Then move the nocking point down $1/16''$ at a time until the variance increases again. Compare the recorded variances and set the nocking point to the location with the smallest variance.

Focusing on the Plunger Tension

1. Have your archers hang their targets with the line running vertically.
2. Have your archers shoot six arrows down the tape while concentrating on keeping their sight pins on the tape. We don't care about our spacing up and down, only our windage and staying on the line.
3. Pull any bad shots out of consideration and then measure the group variance/width left to right; record the variance.
4. Have them add $1/4$ turn (clockwise) to the plunger tension and then repeat the exercise recording the change and the variance for each new location. If the variance decreases continue adding tension to the button until the variance increases.
5. Then reduce the plunger tension $1/4$ turn (counterclockwise) at a time until the variance increases again. Compare the recorded variances and return the plunger to the tension with the smallest variance.
6. To complete fine tuning of the plunger, start this exercise over at this setting recording the variance.
7. Have them add $1/8$ turn to the plunger tension and then repeat the exercise recording the change and the variance for each new setting. If the variance decreases continue adding tension to the button until the

variance increases again.

8. Then reduce the plunger tension $^1/_8$ turn at a time until the variance increases again. Compare the recorded variances and return to the setting with the smallest variance.

Fine Tuning for Outdoor Competition

Normally, by the time we move outdoors with each new crop of kids we have almost lost our minds. While I love shooting indoors, for about 30 minutes, I am always anxious to get outdoors where the greatest challenges and opportunities await. One opportunity that awaits us outdoors is the chance to finally do some serious tuning. We always want to make sure that we spend our last week of indoor shooting switching over to outdoor equipment, making all the normal adjustments and then tuning the outdoor equipment indoors. When we head outdoors we have everybody and everything ready to rock 'n' roll. If that's the case then the first thing I want to do outdoors, tuning wise, is the French Method, also known as the Walk Back Method.

The French/Walk Back Method

Preparation for testing with the French or Walk Back Method includes having them all get a sight setting for 10 meters and finding or setting up a buttress that will accommodate their needs for about a 6 ft / 2 m group, top to bottom. If you aren't fortunate enough to have a backstop of those dimensions an easy option is to set one 48″/52″ matt on the ground in front of another matt already mounted on a target stand. Before shooting be sure to secure the second matt to the stand in a manner that will prevent the second matt from falling over on their arrows. While we may not need all of them, mark distances from 10 to 70 meters from the target at 10-meter increments. Now install an aiming spot or a small target near the top of the upper target matt.

Have your archers perform this exercise one at a time to avoid confusion.

1. Set their sights on the 10-meter mark
2. Aiming all shots at the target or aiming spot and without changing their sights have them shoot an arrow from the 10-meter line, 20-meter line, 30-meter line and so on backing up as far as they can without shooting an arrow so low as to miss the available space on the target matts.
3. Have your archers shoot an extra shot to replace any bad shots that they may shoot in the process remembering to pull the bad shots from the group before analysis.

The Analysis

1. Archers who are skilled enough to benefit from this exercise will find their arrows fit into one of five basic group patterns.

2. Pattern #1, straight line top to bottom, is most desirable and indicates that "All Systems are Go" and that no adjustment to button position or tension is required.

3. Pattern #2, diagonal line to the left top to bottom, is an indication that the button is too stiff. (RH archer/reverse for LH)

4. Pattern #3, diagonal line to the right top to bottom, is an indication that the button is too soft. (RH archer/reverse for LH)

5. Pattern #4, curved line to the left top to bottom, is an indication that the button is not protruding far enough to the left. (RH archer/reverse for LH)

6. Pattern #5, curved line to the right top to bottom, is an indication that the button is protruding too far to the left. (RH archer/reverse for LH)

7. There is a 6th Basic Group pattern which I will simply refer to as the spray. That pattern, actually the lack of any discernable pattern, is simply an indication that this archer is not ready for this test.

See diagram at right.

Fine Tuning With the Bare Shaft Method

I have said before that many archers, including me, take this method a little farther when they go outdoors. In fact, in final preparation for an outdoor tournament I like to shoot my bare shaft with my group at the longest distance I will be shooting, but please don't take your kids straight to 70 meters to do their tuning. You had them tune with a bare shaft at 10 and then 20 meters indoors. So, use the same responsible technique outdoors. Have them tune with the Bare Shaft Method at 30 meters first and when you think they are ready allow them to tune at 40 meters and so on until the ones who are able have reached their tournament distance.

It is a bit of a confidence builder when they can shoot their bare shafts in a group at a distance like 70 or 90 meters. They may just start thinking that their shots are clean enough and their bows are tuned well enough that they are ready to move up in the rankings.

There are many more things to look at going forward to optimize their set-ups. Just in the world of bowstrings I would like to spend more time testing new bowstring materials, number of strands, different brace heights and how they affect performance. Simple exercises that we used to test our nocking point and button tension can be repeated with the string variables I mentioned and we would all benefit from this information. However, practice time is limited, so I have tried to hit the most important factors having an impact on your team's success and hope that it serves you and your shooters well.

The French or Walk Back Tuning Patterns

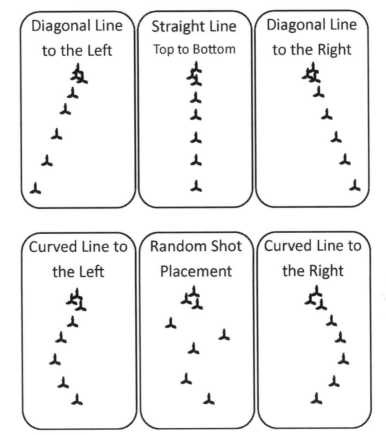

Diagonal Line to the Left

Straight Line Top to Bottom

Diagonal Line to the Right

Curved Line to the Left

Random Shot Placement

Curved Line to the Right

Bob Ryder

Equipment — Compound

Getting a bow that can be adjusted to your archer's current needs and their future needs is paramount. This is JMU archer Caroline McCracken at full draw at the 2019 U.S. National Outdoor Collegiate Championships.

22

Equipment Selection for New Compound Archers

The landscape of collegiate archery competition has changed a lot over the years. When I competed in college, 1969-74, everyone shot a one-piece wooden recurve bow with only the most basic accessories. Recurve remained the only recognized division in college until 1995 when I forced the hand of the College Division by adding full recognition of a compound division at the National Outdoor Collegiate Championships I was hosting at JMU in Harrisonburg, VA even though it had been slated as a demonstration sport only for the second year in a row. Since that time, the College Division has seen consistent growth in the numbers for both Compound and Recurve competitors. While our collegiate nationals had 200 competitors (recurve only) in the early 1970's that number had dwindled to 64 in 1993 when I took my first team to nationals. In 2017 the number competing in the National Championship exceeded 400 archers (recurve and compound).

With the growth in the numbers of compound archers in the college division there has been a corresponding growth in the need for collegiate coaches who could provide help and guidance to those compound archers. I enjoy working with both compound and recurve archers and I find the addition of compound equipment both simpler and more complicated at the same time. I will say that coaching both at the same time really keeps you on your toes. There are many times when you are trying to make a general statement to the group and you'll realize that it only applies to recurve or only to compound so think before you speak and break them into groups when necessary to make sure you don't confuse any of your archers.

Coaching compound archers requires you to do many of the same things as coaching recurve archers. My number one priority is still to recruit the best and most experienced compound competitors you can and build the rest. One difference is that there are a lot more kids on campus who have shot a compound than a recurve primarily because of bowhunting with family or friends. Now this experience can be good or bad, but until you check them out count this experience as an asset that provides some hope for the future.

Check out the New Talent

You start working with your new untested compound archers and often times you recognize that while you never give up on an archer you may have to give up on some of the equipment he comes with. The experienced archers you've recruited are tournament ready and already have all their own equipment. While some of that equipment may require tweaking here and there, your brand-new archers and your hunters are in a different category and will benefit from a discussion on equipment. Let them watch your experienced shooters and explain the features on the equipment that they are using and how that compares to the equipment that they currently have. When they understand the limitations that they will face trying to compete with what they currently own they will probably be ready to pay attention right along with the new folks who have no equipment at all when you start to talk about selecting equipment.

Recommending Compound Equipment

When your students are properly motivated you are again forced to ask that ever important question, "What's your budget?" The difference on the compound side of your team is that the availability of equipment is much better. There seems to be an unlimited supply of compound bows that will serve your purpose. You can buy new equipment from thousands of archery shops across the country. You can buy used equipment from many of those same pro shops or from the many websites set up to connect archers with the equipment others are wanting to upgrade from. Another good source is to make friends with pro-staff or sponsored shooters who have to switch to new equipment every year and eventually figure out that they need to find new homes for their old equipment. You can generally count on this equipment being top shelf and maintained in excellent condition.

Make sure you are zeroed in on the right price range before you get too deep into the search so you can help your archers find a set-up they can have confidence in that doesn't bust their budget. Building an archer's confidence in his ability to perform includes putting an equipment package together that she can have full confidence in. Your help in the selection, set-up, and tuning of that equipment plays a huge roll in giving your archers the confidence they need to compete successfully.

Recommending a Bow

There is a staggering number of compound bows on the market at this time making a new archer's eyes roll back in their head when they try to pick one out of the crowd. There are a slew of manufacturers and each has quite a few choices in their line. It's important to recognize that they offer all these choices to cater to the different needs of their customers. Some bows are designed for hunting, some for 3-D competition, some for target competition, and some designed to crossover a couple of disciplines.

So, with all these choices on the market, how do we hope to provide the right direction to our archers. While we can easily recognize that with new equipment price often provides a general indication of the quality of the equipment, let's not be bow snobs and think that we can only successfully shoot one of the top two brands. It is most important to focus on the features of the bow to determine its suitability for our purposes. While these recommendations are made to provide the best pre-purchase guidance I can give, it does not mean that if the bow a student has doesn't meet some of the specs listed below that it can't be shot well. These recommendations are designed to give your compound archers their best shot and a good archer can and will overcome many obstacles on their way to greatness.

Features to Consider

1. **Length: 37" to 40+"**
   Longer axle to axle lengths tend to be smoother and more consistent (less critical) while shorter length compounds provide the advantage of maneuverability for bowhunters and better clearance in tree stands.

2. **Brace Height: 7" to 8"**
   Taller brace heights tend to be a little slower and a bit more forgiving while shorter brace heights maximize the power stroke and provide more speed to 3-D shooters and bowhunters alike.

3. **Eccentrics: Less Aggressive to Moderate Cams**
   Speed – Slower to moderate speed eccentrics are smoother and more consistent – favoring target archers while the Faster/More aggressive cams better meet the needs of 3-D shooters and bowhunters looking for more speed.

4. **Letoff**
   Elite target archers benefit from letoffs in the range of 60-70% which aids in their ability to hold and aim steadily and produce a repeatable shot while hunters enjoy the benefit of letoffs as high as 90% to allow them to hold at full draw longer while waiting for game to step into a more perfect position.

5. **Draw Stops**
   I can't stress enough the need to have a positive draw stops/string brakes

on both eccentrics. While it is a positive feature for all compound shooters it is critical to the success of a target archer.

6. **Grip: Slim & Low to Medium**

Repeatability is what we are looking for in a grip and with all this letoff it seems that skinny little grips are harder to torque than the larger more comfortable grips that you find on some hunting models.

7. **Limb Quality**

While limbs end up being the single most important component determining performance in a recurve bow the same cannot be said for compounds. The real key to the performance of a compound bow is the design of the eccentrics. You can find out how well a new bow will perform by adding the new eccentrics to solid glass limbs or heck even using the oak slats out of an old shipping pallet, as long as they were trimmed to the right size. Bear Archery discovered years ago that the fiberglass leaf springs from auto manufacturers made great bow limbs. Now that I've made all the manufacturers mad I will say that the true value of all the research, design, and improving manufacturing techniques on bow limbs is in the durability and reliability of the higher end limbs being manufactured today. Always buy the best you can afford because the manufacturers are working hard to provide the best most innovative products they can build.

8. **Mass/Weight: More Please**

While you have to be able to hold it up to aim, mass/weight is your friend when it comes to aiming, holding in the wind, and overall stability. If you select an ultra-light bow you will just end up adding more stabilizer weights to your set-up to make it work for you. Just realize when you see the bows offering lighter mass weights they are generally targeting the hunting market where portability can be a real advantage.

Right- or Left-Handed?

Hopefully, you will be working with this new archer for an extended period of time, maybe even four years, you should choose their bow based on your eye dominance test.

Since you will be having your students use a peep sight with their compound bows you have more flexibility. It is much easier to ignore the dominant eye when using a peep site due to the fact that you are only looking through the peep with one eye. So, while we like knowing the dominant eye and working with it when we can, the peep site is a game changer and gives us the flexibility to make the decision that best serves the archer in question.

What Draw Weight?

We are aided here by the limitation of 60# for the draw weight of compounds being shot in World Archery/USA Archery competitions. Ideally, the bow that you recommend to your new archer has a top end weight appropriate for competition and enough range of adjustment to crank down to a weight that is light enough to allow the development of good form based on both your archer's current strength and anticipated development. The last thing you want is an archer who is over bowed or trying to shoot a weight before they are ready. Remember, they must be able to draw the bow under control when shooting archery tournaments. If an official sees an archer looking like a contortionist when drawing their bow or drawing their bow at an unsafe angle they will be asked to step off the line, make whatever adjustment must be made to draw safely or withdraw from the competition. So please put them in the right weight and teach them the proper technique to draw the bow from the beginning.

What Accessories?

The accessories you will need to complete the set-up process and have your new compound archer ready to shoot include:

1. *Arrow Rest* While there seem to be thousands of choices on the market all you really want an arrow rest to do is exactly the same thing every time while allowing for proper vane clearance. You can get it done reasonably with a simple rest with a fixed launcher blade. You can make it work for different arrows simply by changing launcher blades.
   a. 0.008″ thickness for arrows under 325 grains
   b. 0.010″ thickness for arrows 325 to 425 grains
   c. 0.012″ thickness for arrows over 425 grains
   If their budget can handle it, stepping up to rest models with micro-adjustability for both vertical and horizontal movements is a big plus.

2. *Bow Sight* This is the one place where I would encourage your archers to invest in the best they can afford. There is a lot going on with a sight and while you can shoot a good score with a cheap sight you will eventually lose your mind trying to keep all the screws tight and fixing your sight because it vibrates into a new location. Shooting an extended sight with a scope only compounds your sight problems since the energy exchange on the release shocks the scope on every shot. While occasionally the small threaded rod which extends from the scope housing to the sight block actually breaks, the normal result is to vibrate loose every screw and bolt connected to the sight. Basically, the sight manufacturers will say that you can pay me now or pay me later but you will eventually have to get a good

sight. I can recommend Axcel or Shibuya.

3. *Telescopic Aperture (aka "Scope")* A lot of aperture options exist and there are some reasonable options that will provide your students an advantage over shooting with just a pin. I recommend they start out with a smaller, 1⅜", scope housing for maximum clearance and limited vibration. They should also start out with a 2-power lens in their scope and get used to that before deciding to go up in power. When they are ready to spend more money, the options are to improve the quality of the lens they shoot for greater clarity and higher end scope housings to improve the stability and durability of the entire scope.

4. *Peep Sight* While discussions on the peep sight could consume an entire book I like to start the kids out with a simple Tru-Peep, with ¹⁄₃₂" or ³⁄₁₆" holes. Naturally, as soon as they can afford it there are many options to consider such as a hooded peep housing with interchangeable apertures.

5. *Stabilizer* This is another area where while you will want your archers to have the best when they can afford it, they can find some real savings in buying one of the low-end to mid-range options.

6. *Release Aid* Professional archers who make their living based solely on their performances in target archery competitions will normally show up with an assortment of triggerless (*aka* back tension) and thumb trigger handheld releases because they give them the most consistent performance day in and day out. That being said, the fastest way from 0 to 560 on the indoor double FITA I is to start your kids out on a good wrist caliper release aid at less than half the price of those fancier handheld models. They're simple, consistent, and inexpensive and will serve them well until they develop a solid shooting form. Once they are ready for the challenge and extra expense they take the next step.

Recommending Arrows

Since we start our new kids off indoors when they buy their equipment we give them the option of buying indoor arrows to get started and their outdoor arrows later as we get closer the outdoor season or they can choose to buy their outdoor arrows right off the bat to shoot year-round.

1. *Indoor* Some of the easiest and most reasonable options are still aluminum shafts for indoors. We recommend everything from Platinum Plus to X-7's for our compound shooters depending on their budgets. I will continue to watch for good indoor options from the many all carbon arrows that are targeting that market now. Currently we find that PS-23's and XBusters are good choices for all-carbon indoor arrows.

2. *Outdoor* Obviously, I'd like to have all my kids shooting X10's outdoors but

budgets force most into ACG's or ACC's. I look forward to giving the excellent options from Gold Tip, Black Eagle and Carbon Express a more serious look in the future.

Recommending Other Accessories

They will need many other accessories that are much less critical to their success where not much guidance is required. Below you will find a list of equipment recommended for all Compound archers including equipment that is required to be able to shoot and those items that are optional (marked "Optional").

Recommended Equipment List for Compound Target Archers

Bow
    Compound Bow
    Sight
    Scope
    Arrow Rest
    Stabilizer w/weights
    Side Mount (Optional)
    Side Rod w/weights (Optional)
String
    Peep Sight
    String Loop
    Kisser Button (Optional)
Personal
    Release Aid
    Armguard
    Bow Sling (Bow/Finger or Wrist)
    Chest Protector (Optional)
Arrows (Indoor)
    Shafts (Aluminum/Carbon/Aluminum-Carbon)
    Points
    Nocks
    Fletches (Feathers or Vanes)
Arrows (Outdoor)
    Shafts (Aluminum-Carbon or Carbon)
    Points
    Nocks
    Fletches (Vanes)
Miscellaneous

Quiver
Miscellaneous (con't)
  Arrow Puller (Optional)
  Arrow Lube (Optional)
  Bow Stand (Optional)
  Bow Case (Soft/Hard)
  Optics – Binoculars and/or Scope & Tripod (Optional)
  Rain Gear (Optional)
  Waterproof Shoes/Boots (Optional)
  Bow Square (Optional)
  Allen Wrenches (Optional)
  Bow String Wax (Optional)
  Dental Floss (Optional)

The sheer numbers of choices available in compound bows and accessories are mind boggling and new and better options are being invented as I write this. But, I hope this brief offering will help you to better guide your new archers into equipment choices that will make sense for them as they embark on their journey and pursue their dreams of standing on the top of the podium.

*Checking peak draw weight is a must; here Coach Darryll Diehl is
checking that of a team member's bow.*

23

Basic Set Up for a New Compound Bow

Our goal in setting up a new compound is aimed at establishing the proper set up for the average archer. The bow will be set up within generally acceptable measurements to start and will be modified to provide better performance and more forgiveness during the tuning process once the archer has demonstrated consistent form and grouping.

Steps of Setting up the Compound Bow

1. *Check Tiller* by using your bow square to measure the distance from the base of the top limb, where it attaches to the riser, to the string at its closest position. Then measure the distance from the base of the bottom limb, where it attaches to the riser, to the string at its closest point. Subtract the measurement recorded for the lower limb from the measurement recorded for the upper limb to get your tiller measurement as it is most commonly referred to, i.e. $+1/8''$ The most commonly acceptable tiller on a compound bow is Zero (even tiller). This is just the starting point but it's a good starting point and works out well for a two-wheel compound which Tom Jennings referred to as a "self-balancing system."

2. *Set Tiller* by using your Allen Wrench. For this exercise, I will assume we want to shoot an even tiller but our initial measurement is $+1/16''$ and that you want to maintain the draw weight the bow is set at.

   a. First, determine if your bow is equipped with limb bolt locks. If it has limb bolt locks loosen the set screws that lock the limb bolts.

   b. Next, add $1/4$ turn onto the top limb bolt while taking $1/4$ turn off the bottom limb bolt.

   c. Check the tiller again. Repeat process until the tiller is at your desired measurement.

   d. Normally, we would now tighten the set screws but in the initial set up we will move right on to checking the draw weight.

3. ***Check Bow Draw Weight*** by
   a. Drawing the bow to full draw with a bow scale and then letting the bow down and reading the recorded weight.
   and
   b. Then having the student pull the bow to see if it is a manageable weight.
4. ***Set the Bow's Draw Weight*** to the desired weight by adjusting the limb bolts with your Allen wrench. While there are some variations between manufacturers I will provide directions for the majority. For this example, we will assume we need to reduce the draw weight four pounds (4#).
   a. First, use your Allen wrench to take two turns off each of your limb bolts by rotating the limb bolts counterclockwise.
   b. Check the draw weight again. If you reduced the weight 3 of the 4# try backing another $\frac{2}{3}$ to $\frac{3}{4}$ of a turn off each bolt and check again. Keep making adjustments until to reach your desired weight.
   c. Next, if your bow is equipped with limb bolt locks, tighten the set screws that lock the limb bolts.
5. ***Install the Front Stabilizer.***
6. ***Stand the Bow*** up using the front stabilizer and leaning the bow against an arrow as upright as possible.
7. ***Establish a Centershot*** reference by using a pair of limb gauges or
   a. Installing pieces of tape on the top and bottom of each limb where they attach to the riser and near the eccentrics.
   b. Measure the width of the limb and mark the center of the limb on the pieces of tape nearest the eccentrics.
   c. Sighting across the bow make a new mark on the tape where the string comes out of the eccentrics.
   d. Measure the distance between the two marks.
   e. Measure the width of the limb and mark the center of the limb on the pieces of tape where they attach to the riser.
   f. Add a second mark on the pieces of tape nearest the riser that reflects the distance between the two marks we measured earlier.
8. ***Install the Arrow Rest*** at a position with the point of contact with the arrow and the rest directly over the pivot point of the bow where the brace height is measured from.
   a. Adjust the windage of the launcher arm on the rest so that when you look across the string the center of the arrow rest lines up with the second lines you drew on the tape. Note This is how the set up recognizes and compensates for the eccentrics positioning the string and string cable outside of the true center of the bow.
   b. Snap a completed arrow that your student plans to shoot with this bow

on the string at a location approximately level with the top of the rest attachment hole.

 c. Adjust the elevation of the launcher arm on the rest till the center of the arrow sets even with the center of the rest mounting bolt, keeping the rest at an angle of 30-35 degrees above level.

9. *Mark the Nock Location* for your student's nocking point with a black or silver Sharpie (depending on the color of the serving) with the plan to have the arrow at a 90-degree angle with the string. This normally means top of the nock being located between $\frac{1}{16}''$ & $\frac{3}{16}''$ above level depending on the size of the arrow and how much the launcher flexes when the arrow is placed on the rest.

10. *Install a D-loop* at the location marked above. I prefer the version with the loop tied both above and below the nock location allowing us to pull from directly behind the nock. Note This allows the archer to draw and let down the bow without requiring the nock to be reseated. But even more importantly, on release, the string drives the arrow straight forward avoiding the forces from other directions as experienced when using single location D-loops which have initial contact only on the top or bottom of the nock.

11. *Install the Sight* onto the bow. As there are many variations of sight attachments I will simply make a couple of suggestions.

 a. Install your sight mounting block with the manufacturer supplied screws. Since these screws like to vibrate loose save yourself some trouble by using a drop of LocTite *Thread Locker (Blue)* on each of the mounting screws for a little piece of mind. While you can still easily remove them with an Allen wrench they will generally never vibrate loose.

 b. After completing the assembly of the sight lean the bow up on an arrow again, get in position to look down the string and arrow again, and set the sight so the scope is directly over the center of the arrow as it sets on the rest. While you may not be able to set the sight for your new archer this should give him a good starting point left and right.

 c. Level the sight to the bowstring at this time but you can easily save the adjustments to the 2nd and 3rd axes for later such as when your archer is ready to tune.

12. *Set the Draw Length* to fit your archer properly. Hopefully, your student has purchased a bow that is the correct draw length and if so, it is either right as it sits or you will simply need to adjust or change the draw modules as necessary by following the manufacturer's instructions. Make sure as you finalize the draw length for your archer that you have the string on the tip of their nose when they go to their anchor. If they draw to the side of their nose either make an adjustment to their form or to their bow's draw

length to make this happen. This small thing will make them a more successful archer and you a more successful coach.

13. *Check Eccentric Timing* by pulling the bow to full draw and paying close attention to the rollover of the cams and when you arrive at the wall for top and bottom cams. If you are fortunate enough to have your draw tap the walls or draw stops at the same time then you're done. If one taps earlier than the other then you will need to make a small adjustment to your timing.

14. *Adjust the Timing* of the eccentrics by
   a. Determining which of the cams reaches the draw stop first. For our purposes, we will say it is the top cam.
   b. While focusing on the other (lower) cam, flex the buss cable and watch to see the lower cam advance. Once you have confirmed that shortening the buss cable advances the correct (lower) cam move to the next step.

   c. Place the bow in the bow press and take the tension off the cables.
   d. Remove one end of the bus cable you confirmed in step b) and add one full twist to the cable.

Check the timing of the eccentrics during the set-up of a new compound.

   e. Reinstall the buss cable and put the tension back on the cables.
   f. Draw the bow again and check the timing. If the timing is good you are done and if it's closer but not perfect try the same thing again. If the movement caused the bottom cam to advance ahead of the top cam then take one half twist out and try again.

15. *Install the Peep Sight* I want you to take your time on this one. Naturally, if you are setting up a bow for an experienced archer who has already established a solid anchor with muscle memory and a precise contact point, installing the peep site becomes a simple exercise. However, we will assume this is a new archer being set up with a new bow and you will want to spend some quality time with the archer establishing the perfect, repeatable anchor before you try to install the peep.
   a. Establish the anchor point by working with your archer to find the right anchor and having him/her shoot enough arrows to demonstrate the ability to shoot groups without the use of a peep site.
   b. Have your archer draw to their anchor while you observe and if you approve of the anchor mark the string for the peep location.
   c. Place the bow in a bow press to take a little pressure off the string.

d. Install the peep by separating the strands of the string at the location you marked and inserting the peep or peep housing.

e. Tie in the peep with string serving both above and below the peep.

16.*Install the kisser button.* (Optional) A good training tool for new archers that is abandoned by most after developing their form is actually still used by a few advanced archers. The kisser button seems to help new archers find some stability in their anchor as they transition through trying wrist caliper, thumb trigger, and triggerless/back tension releases. Once they gain perfect their anchor and gain some consistency they can remove the kisser button with no adverse side effects.

a. Have your archer draw to anchor several times until you are satisfied they are going to the anchor you recommend.

b. Mark the location for the kisser button.

c. Install the kisser button by

i. *Traditional Kisser Button* Press the button against the string until it pops on. If it is too tight you can slide it onto a small screwdriver first to expand the slot and then slide it off the screwdriver onto the string in the desired location. Then lock it in place by tying it in with serving material.

ii. *Soft Rubber Kisser Button* Put your bow into a bow press and take enough tension off the string to take the string off the top cam, attach a cotter pin like installation tool on the upper string loop, slide the kisser button over the installation tool and down the string to the desired location. Reinstall the string loop onto the top cam. Then lock it in place by tying it in with dental floss or serving material.

iii. Tie on a kisser touch point with serving material.

The bow is now set up well enough to shoot without your archer suffering any self-inflicted injuries. Soon your archer will be shooting consistently and you'll be ready to tune it for even better performance.

Often adjustments to compound bows are easier to make on "the bench." Here Stacy Knighten is making adjustments to an arrow rest on a compound bow.

24
Basic Tuning for Compounds

There's no rest for the weary. As the coach of a college team with both recurve and compound archers you just move from one thing to another. Once you set up equipment for your new recurve archers you have a little break for them to improve their skills and consistency before getting into tuning. However, the minute you finish setting up your kids compound equipment it is the time to move right into paper tuning.

Before we start tuning let's review the major steps we did to set them up originally.
1. Set Tiller – Even
2. Set Centershot – Reflect position of String
3. Set Eccentric Timing – Balanced
4. Set Nocking Point – $1/8''$ Above Level
   From $1/16''$ for small diameter shafts w/Easton G Nocks or equivalent to $3/16''$ for large diameter shafts w/Easton Super Nocks or equivalent

Paper Tuning

When I was an archery manufacturer's representative I used to travel around speaking and shooting demonstrations at bowhunter jamborees and trade shows. I was one of the freaks that gave talks and demonstrated shooting recurves and compounds in the same show. After I started to discuss tuning techniques, when I got to paper tuning I always started out the same way. I would explain that you should take a large picture frame like the one with that old picture of your mother-in-law. Take a hammer and knock the glass and the picture out of it and cover it with paper. Now see, you already feel better about life and we haven't even started tuning your bow. That would normally put the crowd in a good mood and very receptive to the concepts I was about to introduce. We don't need any jokes or fancy tricks to get our kids ready to paper tune. You have earned their trust so far and they are ready for you to take them the next step in the process.

Get out your paper tuner if you have one. If not, you can fashion one out of a picture frame and you will want in mounted so the opening is shoulder height so they can shoot level through the paper into a backstop that is a little taller than shoulder height. Ideally the frame would have an opening 24″ x 24″ but I have successfully used 10″ x 10″ on bows that I did the set up on. The risk when skimping on the size is that if the arrow actually strikes the frame it can be broken or bent beyond repair.

Before allowing your archers to participate in paper tuning make sure their bow hand is relaxed and properly located in the grip. I prefer seeing their fingers curled with the knuckles at a 45-degree angle. But, like Mick Jagger says, "You can't always get what you want, but if you try sometimes . . . you get what you need." And what I need is for the bow hand to be relaxed.

I used to pride myself on being able to take a low poundage compound that was properly tuned and show how I could demonstrate a tear in nearly any direction I wanted just by abusing the grip. This was to help explain to dealers who were being requested to re-tune bows for the fourth time that an ounce of prevention is worth a pound of cure. Make sure the shooter understands how he can sabotage his own set up just by not taking the time to relax and properly locate their hand in the grip.

It's also a good idea to make sure the arrows that your archers will be shooting with to tune with are up to the task. Remember these kids are new archers so don't forget to:

1. *Check the Components* Make sure that all the arrows have the same nocks, fletches and points and that all the components are properly and securely attached. Remove all arrows that do not meet this criteria from the archer's quiver before tuning.

2. *Check for Straightness* Have them spin their arrows and remove arrows from their quivers that do not spin smoothly. If they are unable to spin their arrows to check for straightness then you do it for them.

3. *Check the Indexing of the Nocks* Make sure the nocks on all their arrows are turned to the position which should provide the greatest vane clearance for their set up. Any arrow suffering a hard strike on the way past the arrow rest will not provide the results you are hoping for.

4. *Check the Nock Fit* Arrows with a nock fit that is too tight will prevent you from successfully tuning your archers bow. The nock should snap onto the string but the throat size should allow movement on the serving. Proper nock fit should allow the arrow to hang on the string but easily release from the string when you tap the string with two fingers. Any tighter will distort your tuning results and any looser will result in inconsistency. If the nock is too tight you can try switching from a small groove nock (0.088″) to a

162

large groove nock (0.098″), reserve the bowstring with a smaller diameter serving or switch to a smaller diameter string. If the nock is too loose, temporarily build up the serving under the nocking point with dental floss. If this works satisfactorily then you can reserve the string with a larger diameter serving material.

5. *Check the Draw Weight* Pull out your grain scale and make sure that the arrows you will be using to tune are within about 2 grains of the same weight. Eliminate any real oddballs from this exercise.

    Note We aren't throwing your new archer's arrows away. You can help them bring any rejects into compliance later. But for now, we don't want to move on to the tuning using equipment that will be counterproductive to that process.

The Test

1. Set your paper tuner up three or four feet (1 yard/meter) in front of your backstop. Far enough from the backstop that the arrow clears the paper but not so far that the arrow might escape the backstop.
2. Have your archers stand 3-4 feet in front of the paper tuner.
3. Have them shoot three arrows into the paper spaced out enough that the arrows do not share a tear. You want to make sure that all the arrows have the same tear. If not, the archer needs to work on shooting with more consistent form before actually tuning. While with an experienced archer you may just have them shoot just one arrow, new archers may have a difficult time producing consistent results.
4. Once you have a tear you can trust, it's time to analyze the results.
    See the nock tear diagrams on the next page.

The Analysis of the Paper Test Results

The analysis of the results is based on the tear displayed on the paper tuner. I always work on high or low tears first, saving all left and right tears for once the nocking point has been refined/corrected.

If the size of the tear is fairly small I like to have the archers back up to where the tear is at its greatest. You want to catch the arrow after it clears the bow but before it starts its correction. Often, we find that we get the greatest tear between 5 and 7 yards/meters from the paper tuner and when we make our adjustments there we have our best results.

High Tear

If the nock end of the arrow gives us a high tear it indicates that the nocking point is too high.

Paper Tuning Tear Patterns

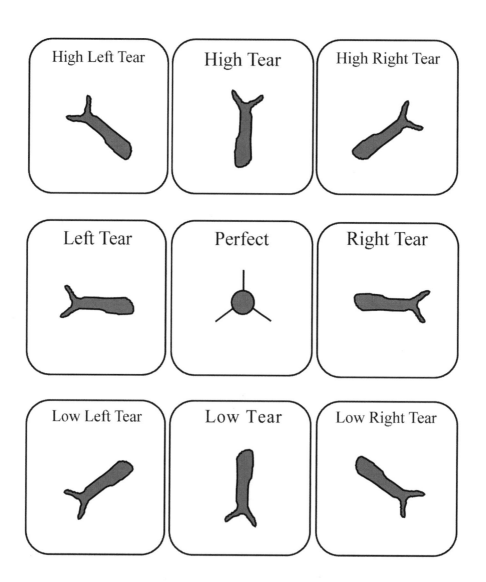

Resolution Lower the nocking point.
Move the nocking point or string loop down ¹⁄₁₆″ and try again. Continue this process until the error in elevation is corrected and the arrow yields a bullet hole or a tear straight right or straight left.

Low Tear

If the nock end of the arrow gives us a low tear it indicates that the nocking point is too low.

Resolution   Raise the nocking point.

Move the nocking point or string loop up $\frac{1}{16}''$ and try again. Continue this process until the error in elevation is corrected and the arrow yields a bullet hole or a tear straight right or straight left.

For Right-Handed Archers

Left Tear

If the nock end of the arrow gives us a left tear it indicates one of two things. The most likely culprit is the rest position being too far to the left but another possibility is an arrow spine that is too weak.

Resolution   Move the arrow rest to the right $\frac{1}{16}''$ and try again. Continue this process until the error is corrected and the arrow yields a bullet hole. If moving the arrow rest does not resolve the issue then you need to resolve the issue of the arrow being under the proper spine.

1. Decrease the bow weight by taking one turn off (counter clockwise) each of the limb bolts and try again. Continue this process until you achieve a bullet hole.
2. Change to a lighter point weight in the arrows and try again. Try different options until the Left Tear is resolved.
3. Cut $\frac{1}{4}''$ off the length of the arrows, assuming you have length to spare, and try again. Continue the process until you produce the tear you are looking for or until you no longer have unnecessary arrow length to spare.
4. Consult an archery pro shop or an arrow spine chart, purchase arrows with a proper spine for the bow and start over.

Right Tear

If the nock end of the arrow gives us a right tear it indicates one of two things. The most likely culprit is the rest position being too far to the right but another possibility is an arrow spine that is too stiff.

Resolution   Move the arrow rest to the left $\frac{1}{16}''$ and try again. Continue this process until the error is corrected and the arrow yields a bullet hole. If moving the arrow rest does not resolve the issue then you need to resolve the issue of the arrow being over the proper spine.

1. Increase the bow weight by adding one turn (clockwise) onto each of the limb bolts and try again. Continue this process until you achieve a bullet hole.

2. Change to a heavier point weight in the arrows and try again. Try different options until the Right Tear is resolved.

3. Consult an archery pro shop or an arrow spine chart, purchase arrows with a proper spine for the bow and start over.

For Left-Handed Archers

Left Tear

If the nock end of the arrow gives us a left tear it indicates one of two things. The most likely culprit is the rest position being too far to the left but another possibility is and arrow spine that is too stiff.

Resolution Move the arrow rest to the right ¹/₁₆″ and try again. Continue this process until the error is corrected and the arrow yields a bullet hole. If moving the arrow rest does not resolve the issue then you need to resolve the issue of the arrow being over the proper spine.

1. Increase the bow weight by adding one turn (clockwise) onto each of the limb bolts and try again. Continue this process until you achieve a bullet hole.

2. Change to a heavier point weight in the arrows and try again. Try different options until the Right Tear is resolved.

3. Consult an archery pro shop or an arrow spine chart, purchase arrows with a proper spine for the bow and start over.

Right Tear

If the nock end of the arrow gives us a right tear it indicates one of two things. The most likely culprit is the rest position being too far to the right but another possibility is and arrow spine that is too weak.

Resolution Move the arrow rest to the left ¹/₁₆″ and try again. Continue this process until the error is corrected and the arrow yields a bullet hole. If moving the arrow rest does not resolve the issue then you need to resolve the issue of the arrow being under the proper spine.

1. Decrease the bow weight by taking one turn off (counter clockwise) each of the limb bolts and try again. Continue this process until you achieve a bullet hole.

2. Change to a lighter point weight in the arrows and try again. Try different options until the Left Tear is resolved.

3. Cut ¹/₄″ off the length of the arrows, assuming you have length to spare, and try again. Continue the process until you produce the tear you are looking for or until you no longer have unnecessary arrow length to spare.

4. Consult an archery pro shop or an arrow spine chart, purchase arrows with a proper spine for the bow and start over.

Paper tuning for compounds is not the end all and be all for perfecting arrow flight and grouping for the compound archer. However, it is a wonderful way to get started with the tuning process.

Clearance Issues

One thing that can throw a monkey wrench into the whole process here is clearance issues. If you find that when you are trying to help your archers paper tune their bows that the tears are not clearing up as described. If you think their form is not the issue you may want to get the foot powder out and check for clearance problems. Spray the arrow fletching then have them shoot a clean shot. Check the arrow for streaks coming from contact with the rest/riser. Try turning the nock to provide better vane clearance and try again. (This is called nock indexing.) Once the clearance problem is resolved you can return to paper tuning with a much bigger chance of positive results.

So far tuning for compounds has been nothing but fun stuff and I can assure you that there are some more tedious tuning techniques out there for you to try. I do share some more advanced tuning techniques with you in another chapter that should give your kids the confidence to take on the world. And that is the result we're looking for, isn't it?

This plaque was given to me on my 60th birthday. It includes an arrow Robinhooded by Daniel Suter and the words "Who needs back tension?" on it.

25

More Tuning for Compounds

We can talk for days about all the cool techniques people have come up with for tuning compound bows but we will focus here on just a few items that I think will give you the best return on the time you invest. That certainly doesn't mean that I discount the value of the techniques not included in this chapter. It simply means that as a team coach being pulled in twenty different directions at one time you owe it to yourself and to your team to focus on whatever will deliver the greatest improvement of the overall team performance rather than spending an inordinate amount of your time with the team working on things with diminishing returns.

Fine Tuning for Indoor Competition

You've got all your compound archers equipment set up within reasonable parameters and helped them to successfully complete paper tuning their bows. Now what we want to do while we are indoors is to help them with another technique to fine tune the nocking point and arrow rest locations. A little tuning exercise I like to call "Taggin' the Line."

Taggin' the Line

Have each of your archers, who are participating in fine tuning, number all their arrows. Then have each of them take electrical tape or painter's tape wide enough to see at 18 m and put it in a straight line across the back side of a target face or a piece of cardboard.

Focusing on the Nocking Point

1. Have your archers hang their targets up with the line running horizontal.
2. Then have them shoot six arrows across the line while concentrating on keeping their sight pins on the tape. We don't care about left and right spacing, only our elevation and staying on the line.
3. Pull any bad shots out of consideration and then measure the group vari-

ance in height, recording the variance.

4. Have them adjust their nocking points/string loops up $^1/_{16}''$ and then repeat the exercise recording the change and the variance for each new location. If the variance decreases continue moving the nocking points/string loops up in $^1/_{16}''$ increments until the variance increases.

5. Then move the nocking points/string loops down $^1/_{16}''$ at a time until the variance increases again. Compare the recorded variances and set the nocking points/string loops to the location with the smallest variance.

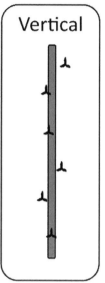

Focusing on the Rest Position
Have your archers hang targets with the line running vertically.

1. Then have them shoot six arrows down the tape while concentrating on keeping their sight pins on the tape. We don't care about our spacing up and down, only our windage and staying on the line.

2. Pull any bad shots out of consideration and then measure the group variance left to right, recording the variance.

3. Have them move their rest $^1/_{16}''$ to the left and repeat the exercise recording the change and the variance for each new location. If the variance decreases continue moving the rest to the left until the variance increases.

4. Then have them move their rest $^1/_{16}''$ to the right and repeat the exercise. Record the variance and if it decreases have them continue the exercise changing the rest location $^1/_{16}''$ at a time until the variance increases again. Compare the recorded variances and return the rest to the location with the smallest variance.

5. To complete fine tuning of their rest positions, start this exercise over at this setting recording the variance.

6. Have them move the rest $^1/_{32}''$ to the left and then repeat the exercise recording the change and the variance for each new location. If the variance decreases continue moving the rest until the variance increases again.

7. Then move the rest $^1/_{32}''$ at a time to the right until the variance increases again. Compare the recorded variances and return to the setting with the smallest variance.

Fine Tuning for Outdoor Competition

Working with your archers over months of indoor practice and competition allows you time to help them develop their skills and muscle memory so when we venture into the great outdoors with greater challenges we will face we can be confident that our students will be up to the challenge.

The French/Walk Back Method

Preparation for testing with the French or Walk Back Method includes having all your students getting a sight setting for 10 meters and finding or setting up a buttress that will accommodate their needs for about a 6´/2 m, top to bottom. If you aren't fortunate enough to have a backstop of those dimensions an easy option is to set one 48˝/52˝ mat on the ground in front of mat already mounted on a target stand. Before shooting please secure the second mat to the stand in a manner that will prevent the second mat from falling over on their arrows. While we may not need all of them, mark distances from 10 to 70 meters from the target at 10 meter increments. Now install an aiming spot or a small target near the top of the upper target mat.

Have your archers perform this exercise one at a time to avoid confusion.
1. Set their sights on the 10-meter mark
2. Aiming all shots at the target or aiming spot and without changing their sights have them shoot an arrow from the 10-meter line, 20-meter line, 30-meter line and so on backing up as far as they can without shooting an arrow so low as to miss the available space on the target mats.
3. Have your archers shoot an extra shot to replace any bad shots that they may shoot in the process remembering to pull the bad shots from the group before analysis.

The Analysis

1. Compound archers who are skilled enough to benefit from this exercise will find their arrows fit into one of three basic group patterns.
2. Pattern #1, straight line top to bottom, is most desirable and indicates that "All Systems are Go" and that no adjustment to rest position is required.
3. Pattern #2, diagonal line to the left top to bottom, is an indication that

Place another butt on the ground in front of the stand to provide a 6' high target to test your set up with the Walk Back Method.

171

the rest is too far to the right. Try moving the arrow rest $^1/_{32}''$ to the left and try the exercise again. Continue until you achieve Pattern #1 (for RH Archer/reverse for LH)

4. Pattern #3, diagonal line to the right top to bottom, is an indication that the rest is too far to the left. Try moving the arrow rest $^1/_{32}''$ to the right and try the exercise again. Continue until you achieve Pattern #1. (for RH Archer/reverse for LH)

5. There is another Basic Group pattern which I will simply refer to as the spray. That pattern or lack thereof is simply an indication that this archer is not ready for this test (*see diagram opposite*).

Taggin' the Line . . . Again

Repeat the Taggin' the Line tuning method outdoors, at the longest distance your archers have shown proficiency at, making the same observations and adjustments that you used indoors but restricting rest movements to $^1/_{32}''$ at a time.

Group Tuning

Have your archers shoot groups at their longest primary distance outdoors, currently 50m for compounds. Assuming they are not already beating their arrows to pieces have them "shoot 'em if they've got 'em." (6-12 arrows to give a full group) During this exercise I want all of each archer's arrows shot. What we are looking for is a nice tight round group for each archer.

What we may see is:

1. Nice tight round group – Bob's happy, you're happy . . . move on.
2. Elongated group left to right – Rest position needs tweaking. Record group size.
   a. Try a $^1/_{32}''$ adjustment to the left and shoot again. If it improves continue until it gets worse, recording the adjustments and the group sizes.
   b. Try a $^1/_{32}''$ adjustment to the right and shoot again. If it improves continue until it gets worse, recording the adjustments and the group sizes.
   c. Return the arrow rest to the position with the smallest group size.
3. Elongated group high to low – Nocking point/string loop position needs tweaking. Record group size.
   a. Move your nocking point/string loop down $^1/_{32}''$ and shoot again. If it improves continue until it gets worse, recording the adjustments and the group sizes.
   b. Move your nocking point/string loop up $^1/_{32}''$ and shoot again. If it improves continue until it gets worse, recording the adjustments and the group sizes.

172

French or Walk-Back Method (Compound)

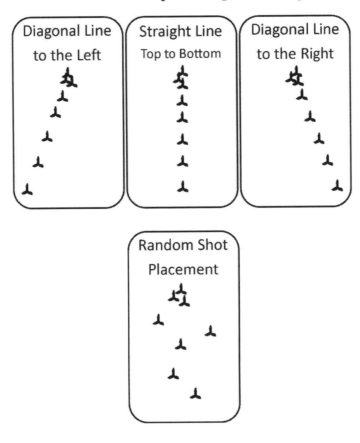

c. Return the return the nocking point/string loop to the position with the smallest group size.

4. Nice tight round group with fliers – The tune is solid but we need to check if the fliers are always the same arrows.
    a. Check the numbers of the fliers and shoot another group.
    b. Check the numbers of the fliers and compare to records
    c. Try turning the nocks of the fliers 120 degrees clockwise and shooting another group. Check fliers again.
    d. Try turning the nocks of the remaining fliers 120 degrees clockwise. Retire the fliers.

    Note Hall of fame compound archer Terry Ragsdale is famous for saying that if an arrow won't join the group after trying three different nock positions that arrow's best use is as a tomato plant stake . . . and I concur.

Just remember. Perfectly tuned equipment alone won't make your kids champions, but what it will do is make sure that the equipment they are using will provide them the greatest advantage possible in their efforts to become the best. Your help in perfecting their shot, properly tuning their bow and fully developing their mental game will eventually put them on top of the podium.

Developing the Mental Game

*JMU archer Brandon Lee struggling at the 2019 U.S. National Outdoor Collegiate
Championships. He was not alone in this. None of us are.*

26

The Mental Game – Why Do They Need One?

There are as many different responses to stress as there are competitors and regardless of whether you have felt the stress of competition yet . . . let me assure you . . . you will.

If you say you haven't felt any stress in competition I would say that you fall into one of the following categories:

1. You have never shot in competition.
2. You have never shot in competition with any personal expectations.
3. You have never shot on a team whose success depended on your performance.
4. You're in denial.

Since at some point in your competitive career you will feel the stress of competition I feel it would be valuable to share with you the responses to stress that I have either experienced or observed in my 50+ years of archery.

Physiological Responses to Stress

- Butterflies
- Elevated Heart Rate
- Perspiration
- Upset Stomach
- Elevated Blood Pressure
- Slight Tremors
- Excessive Perspiration
- Shaking
- Regurgitation
- Loss of Control of Body Functions

Since many of you have not been involved in archery competition to the level and extent that you will experience over the next several years, I want you to think back to the stress or fear you may have experienced in the many other things you have done in your life and see if you can relate to the list above for those experiences.

Some people have the same physiological responses listed above while engaged in the following:

- Auditioning for a Vocal Group or Band
- Trying out for the Basketball Team (or Football, Baseball, etc.)
- Trying out for Cheerleader
- Taking a Test
- Taking the SAT's
- Giving an Oral Presentation
- Being Audited
- Asking a Girl/Boy on a Date
- Getting your Driver's License

In each of these activities your previous actions, practice, preparation or training has set you up to succeed or fail based on your performance or delivery, with someone else being in position to be the judge of your success.

These same feelings and symptoms rear their ugly heads during competition of various types and in archery competition they display themselves with the following results:

♦ Shaking during the Shot
♦ Freezing at Full Draw
♦ Inability to hold on the Gold
♦ Plucking the Release
♦ Dropping the Bow Arm
♦ Breaking Away on Release
♦ Loss of Timing
♦ Loss of Focus
♦ Loss of Concentration
♦ Inability to Pull through the Clicker
♦ Inability to Finish the Shot
♦ Loss of Arrows to the Timing Light
♦ Competitive Performance below Practice Performance

I have seen an archer in an Team Trials event fighting for the last spot on the team throw his bow over his head while saying "I can't take it anymore." Yes, the bow broke and he didn't have to worry about that pressure any more.

I have seen a guy shooting on the fourth and final day of a trials event for an international team who had the last spot on the team sewn up if he could just shoot a 7 on his last arrow at 30 m. Even though he was shooting over a 9.5 average at 30 m he could only manage to shoot a 5 . . . and lost the spot.

After reading the above you guys are probably thinking . . . "Man, this doesn't sound like any fun at all."

The point is . . . that I know the type of things you can go through . . . and I know what you can do to minimize the impact of stress in competition.

Minimizing Stress in Competition

There is not one thing on the lists above that is attractive or desirable during competition so you need to learn the skills to fight the good fight against "nerves" and "stress" that can come with serious competition.

The Mental Game Tools
Focus/Concentration
Controlled Breathing
Progressive Relaxation
Mental Imagery
Positive Self-Talk
Positive Affirmations
Comfort Zones/Resetting Your Thermostat
Managing Conscious Thoughts – During the Shot

We will address these tools one at a time. Please make the effort to better prepare yourself for what is to come because the experiences that await you in your competitive journey will be all the sweeter with the right preparation.

And . . . this being said, you stand there and ask for questions or comments and your team simply asks, "Can we shoot now?"

The beauty of this is while everyone just wants to shoot at the time, those who have enough experience to relate to what you were saying now start coming up to you, one at a time, to discuss with you how to get started. That's the initial reward for your courage.

The seeds you have planted . . . and now the games begin. You are about to start the process of developing archers who are more complete and truly ready for competition.

This photo is of former JMU archer Jacob Wukie wearing his 2012 Olympic Silver Medal. During a team recruitment effort Jacob shared his goal of making the U.S. Olympic Team and who doesn't like a story with a happy ending?

27

The Mental Game – Setting Goals

Before you introduce your team to the Tools of Mental Training you need to spend some time on goals. One thing that everyone should be in agreement on is that "your goals are only dreams until you establish a written plan to accomplish them."

Getting an Initial Commitment

As a coach you are concerned about more than just the competitive success of your archers and that is why I like to start off each year with a group meeting providing a gentle nudge to get them started right. This gentle nudge includes, among other things, the completion of a Confidential Planning Form that includes the opportunity to share their goals with me along with a section where they can briefly communicate their accomplishments for the previous year and their accomplishment-based goals for the next year. In addition, they are required to make three statements concerning their commitment to the team.

1. *The Dream* Where they want to be with their shooting in the future.
2. *The Reality* Where they are right now with their shooting.
3. *The Offer* What they are willing to do to accomplish that goal.

Yes, I realize this is not a very sophisticated method of establishing goals. However, this is how you get a preliminary commitment from 30-40 archers in 15 minutes, and everybody can agree that "a bird in the hand is worth two in the bush." This at least gets them pointed in the right direction from Day One.

You've Got to Believe

What you want to do next is to review the forms that were returned to you and identify the ones that initially seem to be most motivated and set up meetings with them. The more sophisticated establishment of goals with your archers is done face to face with each individual archer and I prefer starting with the ones who have shown the most commitment and motivation on the confidential planning form.

Take a look at the Dream section of their forms. This is where they have the opportunity to share their Ultimate Goal in Archery. For an Ultimate Goal or Dream the sky is the limit. There should be no limitations imposed by you. If anything you should stoke the fire. For maybe the first time in their life I

The Goal Pyramid

want them to reach out for what they really want, not just what they think may be within their reach. They need to understand that this is their goal and that you believe that with enough hard work and dedication they can accomplish anything. Once you have helped them establish their Ultimate Goal the work begins to set Long Term Goals and Short Term Goals to light the path to the top of the podium.

Setting Their Goals

One of your kids decides that his/her goal is to win an Olympic Gold Medal. This to me can logically be listed as his Ultimate Goal.

You then ask him/her, "So what do you have to do to win the Olympic Gold Medal?

1. Make the Olympic Team

   We'll make this our first Long Term Goal. Is there another logical goal that we should meet on our way to our Ultimate Goal? Yes, how about …

2. Earn a spot on the US Archery Team

   We'll make this our second Long Term Goal.

Now we need to ask them "What do we need to do to accomplish these long term goals?" Advise them that we have chosen Outcome Based Goals for our Ultimate and Long Range Goals and while we can we can work diligently toward their accomplishment on a daily basis they are in fact somewhat out of our control and they need to focus their Short Term Goals on actions that are within their control.

While I impose no rules on setting the Ultimate Goal, and the Long Term Goals simply have to be the final stepping stones leading to the Ultimate Goal, we put more structure into the Short Term Goals by introducing them to the concept of SMART Goals.

Establishing SMART Goals

When you sit down with each archer you start out by helping guide them through the process of setting one SMART Goal. The first question they will probably have is "What is a SMART Goal?" Simply stated a SMART Goal is:

S   Specific
M   Measurable
A   Attainable
R   Relevant
T   Time Bound

I believe that the above terms are relatively self-explanatory but if your archers are new to the concept of goals I will describe each briefly. Please note if you need additional guidance after reading the following there seems to no limit to the number of articles, web pages and books that are available discussing the intricate details of defining and setting SMART Goals.

Specific   The goal needs to identify what is to be accomplished in a manner that is clearly understood and offers details where necessary to eliminate the need for interpretation.

For example: If an archer's goal is to "Shoot a 580" I may suggest that the goal should be written to "Shoot a 580 in the Double FITA

1 in tournament by March 31, 2020." If the archer shoots both compound and recurve you would also want to specify the discipline.

Measurable We need to write the goal in a manner that the reader will know not only when it is accomplished. But how much progress has been made towards the goal.

For example: Our goal above to "Shoot a 580 in the Double FITA 1 in tournament by March 31, 2020" is easily measurable and allows an interim evaluation of progress from the archer's current high of 560 toward the goal.

Attainable Our goals, while they should challenge the owner, need to be based in reality.

For example: If our goal above to "Shoot a 580 in the Double FITA 1 in tournament by March 31, 2020" is written by a Barebow archer whose current high is 520 I would consider the goal unattainable. The archer should consider changing the target score or his shooting discipline but I don't think changing the target date would make it much more attainable.

Relevant The goal should be written so that accomplishing it will bring us closer to our Ultimate Goal.

For example: While our goal above to "Shoot a 580 in the Double FITA 1 in tournament by March 31, 2020" will not automatically earn you a spot on the US Archery Team or the Olympic Team I believe that it is relevant in that it is working toward establishing in the archer's own mind his elite status in the sport legitimizing his Long Range Goals.

Time Bound Whatever their goal is they should establish some time table for accomplishing it or a date when it needs to be completed or accomplished.

For example: My goal above to "Shoot a 580 in the Double FITA 1 in tournament by March 31, 2020" clearly establishes the date the goal is to be accomplished and includes the added bonus that the date range includes all of the seasons major indoor tournaments including the National Indoor Championship for the year in question.

Set as many Short Term Goals as necessary to help your archers clearly mark the path to their success.

Now That We Know Where We're Going ... How Do We Get There?

Go ahead and take a look at that Confidential Planning Form (below). Remember me mentioning "The Dream," "The Reality" and "The Offer"? After we use "The Dream" to help establish our archers Ultimate and Long Term

Goals we turn our attention to "The Reality" and "The Offer" as we consider the items to include in their Action Plan.

Each Short Term Goal your archers develop should be accompanied by an Action Plan that is appropriate to the goal. The Action Plan should include the consideration of the items listed in "The Offer".

1. Cardio Training
2. Weight Training
3. Mental Training
4. Form Training
5. Understanding Equipment
6. Learning Tuning
7. Increasing Arrow Count
8. Practicing in Windy Conditions
9. Practicing in Rain/Sleet/Snow
10. Other

When developing an Action Plan don't hesitate to break it down. One item on the Action Plan related to form could be as simple as:

1. "I will execute proper Followthrough on 100% of my shots" or
2. "I will execute 95% of my shots within three seconds."

Getting your team to expand their dreams in archery into written goals is not rocket science but it is important. Don't let any self-imposed rules intended to formalize the process prevent you from getting the job done. Sophisticated is nice for the paperwork and should always be a consideration but more important is getting the goals in writing and putting an effective plan in motion to help them reach the goals that will make them and your entire team successful.

See next page for a sample Confidential Planning Form to help in this process.

JMU Archery Team
Confidential

Name _____ Date _____

Overall Academic & Life Goals

Archery Goal _____
(What is your ultimate goal in archery?)

Career Goal _____
(What do you plan to be doing
for a living in 20 years?)

Degree Goal _____
(What is your major? And do you plan to
pursue an advanced degree?)

Personal Goal _____
(Optional – Share whatever
personal goal you wish to work on.)

Collegiate Goals

Competition	Join Club	Make Team	All-East	All-American	Top 3	Nat'l Champ	World Champ
2019 Accomplishments							
2020 Goals							
Academic	2.0 GPA	2.5 GPA	3.0 GPA	3.25 GPA	Dean's List	President's List	Other
2019 Accomplishments							
2020 Goals							

(con't on next page)

The Dream
Restate your ultimate goal in Archery from above.

_____

_____

The Reality
Describe briefly where you think you are right now with your shooting.

_____

_____

The Offer
What are you willing to do to make your dream become a reality. (Circle)
1) Cardio Training
2) Weight Training
3) Mental Training
4) Form Training
5) Understanding Equipment
6) Learning Tuning
7) Increasing Arrow Count
8) Practicing in Windy Conditions
9) Practicing in Rain/Sleet/Snow
10) Other _____

_____

This is JMU archer Billy Crowe displaying great focus and concentration at the 2019 U.S. National Outdoor Collegiate Championships.

28

The Mental Game – Focus/Concentration

The wonderful television coverage that we all enjoyed during the 2012 Olympic Archery competition provided us an excellent opportunity to experience the competition in a way never before possible. We were able to see, up close and personal, the struggles and triumphs of the world's greatest archers during the most stressful conditions imaginable on the world stage.

Regardless of which tools from the list below the archers may have used in preparation for the games you can be sure that concentration and focus played a major role during the competition.

The Mental Game Tools
Focus/Concentration
Controlled Breathing
Progressive Relaxation
Mental Imagery
Positive Self-Talk
Positive Affirmations
Comfort Zones/Resetting Your Thermostat
Managing Conscious Thoughts – During the Shot

Focus/Concentration

Concentration: the act or process of concentrating, especially the fixing of close, undivided attention.

The key here is to develop the ability to shift your natural recognition of the input provided by all of your six senses to focus on not only the input from one sense but to one specific item with that one sense.

What do I mean? You find yourself at tournament where competition is about to begin and you're eating a banana, you're hearing your favorite new song playing on the PA system, you're watching a really hot archer of the opposite sex putting their bow together, when a draft of air from a barbeque provides you with the most delicious odor you've ever smelled when two blasts of the whistle call you to the line, one blast begins the competition and suddenly you find yourself alone on the line and the only thing you are aware of is the center of the gold on your target as you begin the execution of your first shot. So: tasting, hearing, seeing, feeling, and smelling are reduced to just seeing.

Okay? Well it sounds simple enough and some of your archers will find it easy to do based on your past experience, but others will need to fine tune their ability to concentrate so I have included some exercises I can recommend to develop concentration.

Fine Tune Your Receiver To make this concept easier to understand I want you to recall the last time you were in the practice room. If you are anything like me when you enter the practice room your skills of observation are heightened. You notice everyone who is there, anything interesting that people are wearing, the music being played, if anyone has a new bow or arrows and you hear parts of all conversations and zero in on anyone telling a joke. Observation skills are hitting on all cylinders and since you can put your bow together, complete your warm up stretches and actually start practicing at the same time you are truly putting your incredible skills of multi-tasking on display.

I suggest that all of this is fine until the moment you step to the line. At that time I want the power of concentration to turn everything we just talked about into white noise and you are laser focused to see only the "X" that you are about to destroy.

After all, concentration means that we are focused upon just one thing, to the exclusion of all else. The concentration and focus they develop in order to perfect their shot can be transferred to all other activities that are worthy of their attention. Listening to an important lecture, taking a test, performing surgery or preparing a rebuttal in court.

The point I am so awkwardly trying to make is that this skill is one that will improve their efficiency, effectiveness, and success in many areas of their lives outside of the sport of archery and competition in general.

Learning to Control Your Thoughts The main stumbling block to concentration is the inevitable distraction we get from our own thoughts. It is random, uninvited thoughts that distract you from achieving pure concentration. The only solution is learning to control and quiet your thoughts. The first thing to be aware of is that you do have the choice to welcome or reject those thoughts; you should not feel like a helpless victim of our own mind. If you are trying to execute the perfect shot it is counterproductive to try to think yourself through each of step of the shot while trying to perform. Instead, practice your shooting to the point that the physical actions required to execute the perfect shot are automatic or facilitated. A lobotomy would be good for tournament archers but since that would not be legal. . . . Choose to put something in your mind rather than allowing random thoughts to enter. My all time favorite once I touch my anchor is simply a countdown . . . Three . . . Two . . . One . . . while you finish the shot. It's almost too simple, but it works. Don't concern yourself too much with this concept now as we will revisit it later in another chapter.

Practicing Concentrating Concentration is an activity like any other. Clearly the more we practice it, the better our concentration will become. We wouldn't expect to be a strong runner without doing some training. Similarly, concentration is like a muscle, the more we exercise it the stronger it becomes. There are specific concentration exercises we can do, such as focusing on a small point of an object; but life itself presents innumerable opportunities to sharpen your concentration. The key is to always take opportunities to heighten your power of concentration.

Meditating The practice of meditation will definitely improve your powers of concentration. Actually, when we try to meditate, it is concentration that is the first thing you need to master. A daily period of meditation gives you the chance to work specifically on concentration techniques. This can involve concentrating on your breathing or the relaxation of specific muscles in your body. These exercises are but a start and will be built upon in a future chapter.

Promoting Physical Alertness Our power of concentration depends a lot upon our physical well-being. If we are tired, unhealthy, or distracted by petty annoyances and minor ailments, concentration will be more difficult. Concentration is obviously still possible, it is just more difficult. However, we have to try to make life easy for ourselves; we need to give a high priority to our physical health – getting sufficient sleep and staying physically fit. Establishing an exercise program will help develop our concentration. It will help if we lose excess weight and clear our minds. If we struggle to concentrate, they should work first on improving our physical health and fitness level which will, in turn, help us to develop their power of concentration.

General Concentration Drills
Here are some basic drills to help build their ability to concentrate.

9 Card Drill Take the 2 through 10 of any suit of playing cards and place them face down in random order in three rows. Turn the cards up one at a time to view them briefly. Distract yourself for one minute. Then try to turn the cards over in order, from low value to high. You can increase the difficulty by adding more cards.

The Grid Make a grid, on the computer, 10 columns x 10 rows. Then have someone else fill the grid with numbers from 1 to 100 in random order. Once complete, your drill is to find 1thru 100 in order in the shortest amount of time, checking them off as you find them. Naturally, the best way to do this is with a partner or in a group who shares your goal to improve your focus and concentration. To shorten the timing of this exercise have everyone search for a series of numbers, such as 17 thru 31. Competition with others will drive your improvement.

The Written Word This one you can do by yourself with any book. Open the book to any page and recite the alphabet as you find words that begin with "a" then "b" and so on. I don't care if you don't find an "x" or "z" or if you only go half way through the alphabet. The point is to blast through what you do find as fast as you can without hesitation.

Archery-Specific Concentration Drills

These are archery-specific drills to help build your ability to focus/concentrate.

The Color Drill Put a piece of electrical tape from left to right across a target face right through the middle of the ten. From the normal shooting line go to full draw on the coaches command. After two seconds the coach will call a color and you will shoot at the tape in that color within three seconds. You can also just cut a 3″ wide strip of target, including the gold, to use in the same manner. When you think you've got that down, try straight up and down and for even more fun try it diagonally.

The No Holds Barred Drill You may have heard about the torture we have done to archers at JMU in previous years in the name of training for concentration. It started in the early 1970's when I was on the team. You would go about trying to shoot your normal practice scoring round with an A Line and a B Line. When the A Archers were shooting the B Archers were allowed to distract them in any way they wanted as long as the archer and his equipment were not touched. That meant whispering sweet nothings or blowing in ears, shouting at the archers, calling them names, questioning their value as human beings as well as anything else you could think of to break their concentration. Then when B Archers went to the line the A Archers were allowed to return the favor. This ends up being more of a test than training for improvement but I can tell you that it has helped us more than once in shooting team rounds over the years.

While writing and teaching about concentration and focus is not as cool or sexy as some of the topics in mental training it is an integral part, none the less, and I feel it is important to start here as it is simply one of the most necessary skills to master on our way to the top of the podium.

Breathing between shots is just as important as breathing during shots. This is JMU archer Amelia Nguyen using controlled breathing between shots in the JMU practice room.

194

29

The Mental Game – Controlled Breathing

How easy can this get? You want to teach your kids one of the most valuable tools they can have in their bag for developing their mental game and as with all new tools you need to tell them how much it costs and where they can get it. Now sit-down kids. This tool costs $0 and each human being comes right out of the box with it already pre-installed.

Your students say, "So, what's the trick. What are you talking about?"

We are talking about breathing. We all do it. It's automatic. Even if you hold your breath until you pass out, as soon as you pass out, you automatically start breathing again. Pretty cool, huh? The trick is, for your archers to benefit from breathing in archery competition, they must learn to master controlled breathing.

Once they master it, it will become one of their most valuable tools from the list below that we all need to develop to successfully compete in archery.

The Mental Game Tools
Focus/Concentration
Controlled Breathing
Progressive Relaxation
Mental Imagery
Positive Self-Talk
Positive Affirmations
Comfort Zones/Resetting Your Thermostat
Managing Conscious Thoughts – During the Shot

Interestingly enough, one thing that makes breathing unique is that unlike most bodily functions it is both voluntary and involuntary. All that really means to us at this point is that we can mess around with controlling it voluntarily all we want and when we're done we can be confident that we didn't mess anything up. There is no permanent damage and it goes right back to its default settings.

We address breathing and breath control many times in our instruction but it's only because this tool provides the greatest benefits to them, performance-wise and health-wise, of all the tools on our list. This tool has long been recognized as one of the most effective ways to reduce stress and anxiety naturally, with no drugs required.

So, if controlled breathing is so good for reducing stress, anxiety, blood pressure, and heart rate in normal life, it should be perfect for their use to reduce the stress and anxiety in archery competition. So how do they make it work?

Introducing Breath Control at Practice

Once all your students have arrived at practice tell them you want them to do something a little different tonight and ask them to pair up. Once everybody has a partner teach them to how to take their partners pulse. Make sure if someone ran or biked to practice that you give them time to rest a moment before you proceed. Tell them that they can take their partners pulse by placing their index and middle finger on the inside of their partner's wrist just below their thumb. Count the beats for 30 seconds and then double the number to get the actual beats per minute. Then you record the resting heart rate for each of your students.

Note Make sure that everyone understands not to use their thumb to take the heart rate. Some people don't realize that the thumb has a pulse of its own and will either give you their own heart rate or at least make it harder to figure out.

I went ahead and bought a couple of tools to make the process easier and faster for my practices as an archer and a coach. One item was a Pulse Oximeter which is a really quick and easy way to get your heart rate. Another item I got was the Lumiscope which provides both the heart rate and blood pressure at the same time which will allow for additional insights. No matter how the heart rate is taken it provides an insight into your archers' ability to control their bodies in a manner that will enhance their performance.

Now, keeping the partners together, announce that everyone will be scoring tonight and that you will be posting the scores at the end of the night. Let them shoot two practice ends before they start. After they shoot their second end stop them before they retrieve their arrows and ask everyone to turn in a new heart rate. Let them pull their arrows while you record all the heart rates. You will notice that these heart rates are all elevated over the control rates that

you recorded earlier and explain to them that that is normal and to be expected. But you wanted to prove that point to them tonight before you introduced
them to the topic of Controlled Breathing.

Now that you have their undivided attention, you teach them one of the
most fundamental breathing techniques for relaxation. Explain to them that
all you're going to ask them to do is inhale, hold their breath and then exhale.
Once they acknowledge that that doesn't sound too difficult for them, get a little more specific. Tell them that, to be more specific, you want them to:

1. Inhale a deep breath, on the count of four, through their nose
2. Hold their breath, to a count of two and
3. Exhale slowly, through their mouth, to a count of four

Repeat this breathing three times, then take three deep cleansing breaths on
their pace and then return to normal breathing.

Have them all check their partner's heart rates again for you to record with
the others. You will notice that everyone's heart rate will have returned to normal or below.

You will want to explain that what they just did is a good thing to do any
time before or during a competition to reduce the stress, anxiety or just their
heart rate but that deep cleansing breaths are used by many competitors
between shots to stay relaxed and in control in major competitions.

Arriving at the Competition Venue

You take your team to a competition where you know they want to perform
well. It's good to encourage everyone to take a moment to perform this exercise before they start competing. In fact, you can make it a lot easier for them
to work it into their routine if you have them do the breathing exercises as a
team when they do their team warm-up. That way they won't be so self-con-
scious when they are sitting there doing it alone.

The original introduction to this breathing technique included three cycles
but feel free to reduce it to one or two cycles and see if it doesn't have almost
exactly the same effect.

On the Shooting Line

I recommend you have your archers try the following technique in competition. After they gain experience they will modify this or develop their own
techniques, and that is a good thing.

1. *Take your Stance*
2. *Nock your Arrow* – Deep Controlled Breath & Exhale (90-100%) on 10
   Count (4-2-4)
3. *Raise Bow to Set-Up* – Normal Breath & Exhale (50%)

4. *Draw to Anchor* – Full Normal Inhale to Anchor (50-70%)
or Alternate Method (Inhale Deeply to 90% during draw, exhaling to 50-70%
   by Anchor)
5. *Aiming to Release* – Hold Breath through Release (50-70%)
6. *Follow Through* – Exhale Normally Followed by a Deep Cleansing Breath
   Repeat steps 1-5 until you have shot all your arrows for the end.

I tell them: since the purpose of the Deep Controlled Breaths is to relax you and reduce your heart rate you are welcome to take just one breath or repeat it as your recovery requires and your time allows.

Please explain to them not to go crazy doing overly involved breathing techniques while they are on the shooting line. What is important is for them to try the technique suggested here and then develop their own controlled breathing technique for competition that should include taking at least one deep cleansing breath before each arrow. We just want to keep them calm and relaxed with their heart rate under control.

Other Benefits

It's always nice to read of the other benefits of things we do to become better or more successful archers. These breathing techniques have been recognized for lowering blood pressure along with the heart rate which helps to reduce the risk of strokes or aneurysms. There is even evidence that they help to spark brain growth and even reduce the likelihood or suffering from depression.

Obviously, I don't know what kind of an impact controlled breathing has on anything outside of my field but I believe that it goes a long way to reduce depression brought on as a result of shooting low scores in archery!

And if any of your archers asks you if they really need to take a deep breath before each shot you tell them "Absolutely not! Just the ones you want to be a ten!"

You'd think college students would be experts at relaxation but sometimes they forget this at competitions. This is JMU archer Aaron Sackchewsky relaxing between events at the 2019 U.S. National Outdoor Collegiate Championships.

30

The Mental Game – Progressive Relaxation

My positive approach to the mental game encourages you to have your students keep an open mind to all tools and skills that could potentially provide them an advantage when used independently or in combination with other tools. Progressive Relaxation is a very important tool that you will want your kids to have in their bag because it is extremely valuable even in its most basic form and, when developed to its maximum, will truly unlock the unlimited potential in their minds and bodies for most of life's challenges. Please do not get creeped out by its close relationship to hypnosis. The more you discover about hypnosis the more you will want your students to understand the amazing potential of self-hypnosis and how it differs from what has become the carnival sideshow of stage hypnosis.

The Mental Game Tools
Focus/Concentration
Controlled Breathing
Progressive Relaxation
Mental Imagery
Positive Self-Talk
Positive Affirmations
Comfort Zones/Resetting Your Thermostat
Managing Conscious Thoughts – During the Shot

The relaxation that your archers learned to enjoy and benefit from in the chapter on controlled breathing was just the beginning. By introducing Progressive Relaxation, we will supercharge their ability to relax themselves, slow everything around them down and allow them to take control of their game.

The first thing you will want your team to understand about Progressive Relaxation is just how long it has been around and how widely exercised it is by athletes as well as other folks who just want to win at life. The activities and script that I have written for them here is based on the principles introduced almost 100 years ago by a doctor in Chicago named Edmund Jacobson. While the real strength of his work is the level to which he was able to take the relaxation of specific muscles and muscle groups, I will use this technique simply to introduce to the skill for their use (and yours!) and further development on their own.

The way the system works is for you to have your students to initially tense up muscles/muscle groups one a time, hold the tension for a short time, and then relaxing the tension in the muscles/muscle groups paying particular attention to how the muscles felt through all phases of the activity. Once they have relaxed the first muscle/muscle group you will want them to continue the process with the next muscle group, generally working from head to toes or vice versa.

Now, while I am going to present a script which you will have to read at this time, I recommend that you have your students make audio recordings of the script and play them to themselves while lying in bed to allow themselves to better concentrate on the process.

Basic Progressive Relaxation
Preparation Turn off your lights and eliminate all other distractions including your phone. Lie down on your bed, relax in a recliner or assume whatever comfortable position you may find. As you start to get comfortable resolve any other distractions or discomfort that you may become aware of such as: If your feet are sore then take off your shoes and if you're chilly then put on a blanket. We want everything just right for you.

Progressive Relaxation Script
Lying on your back, let your arms relax down by your side. Now I want you to close your eyes. You will begin to pay attention to your breathing and notice how your abdomen raises and lowers with each breath.

I want you to take a long, slow, deep breath through your nose then slowly and completely exhale through your mouth. When you're ready, take another long, slow breath until you feel your lungs are full and hold this breath for five seconds. As you exhale slowly through your mouth I want you to feel all your troubles and worries flushing right out of your mind and body with the air.

Take another slow, deep breath and again hold that breath for five seconds. Now exhale slowly flushing the last of your worries from your mind in the process.

Now that your mind is free, take one more deep breath, hold for just a second and then let it go. I want you to return to your normal breathing pattern now. At this point you should already feel as if a lot of your tension has left your body.

Take a deep breath and make a fist with your right hand, holding the tension for five seconds. Now exhale as you relax your hand. Notice the differences you feel between tension and relaxation. Continue to relax as you take two more breaths.

Now take a deep breath and make a fist with your left hand, hold the tension for five seconds and exhale as you relax your hand. Continue to relax for two more breaths.

Now let's take a deep breath and make a fist with both hands, holding the tension for five seconds and then exhale as you relax your hands.

Relax for two more breaths.

Now take a deep breath and hold it for five seconds while tensing the muscles in your right foot and calf. Then exhale slowly and relax the muscles. Relax with two breaths. Take another deep breath and hold it for five seconds while you tighten the muscles in your left foot and calf and then exhale slowly while you relax the muscles. Relax with two more breaths. Now take another deep breath and tighten the muscles in both feet and calves. After holding your breath and the muscle tension for another five seconds breath out slowly and relax your muscles.

Relax for two more breaths.

Focusing on your thighs, take a deep breath, hold it and tense up your right thigh, holding it for five seconds, then slowing exhaling while relaxing the right thigh. Take a deep cleansing breath. Take another deep breath and hold it for five seconds while tensing your left thigh. Now exhale slowly while relaxing your left thigh. Take two more cleansing breaths. Take another slow deep breath, hold it for five seconds while you tense both thighs, and then exhale slowly while you relax both thighs. Notice the incredible difference you feel when large muscles are tensed and then relaxed.

Relax for two more breaths.

Moving next to the buttocks, using the same technique take a deep breath and tense the muscles in the buttocks. Hold the tension along with your breath for five seconds and then relax the buttocks. Take two breaths to relax. Take another deep breath and tighten the buttocks while you hold your breath for five seconds. Exhale slowly as you relax your buttocks all the time recognizing a deepening relaxation.

Relax for two more breaths as you move your attention to your stomach.

Draw in a deep breath and tighten your stomach muscles as you hold your breath for five seconds. Try to touch your belly button to your backbone, now relax and exhale the breath. Relax for two more breaths.

Take another deep breath and tighten your stomach muscles again. Hold the tension and the breath for five seconds and then relax and exhale enjoying the relief of complete relaxation.

Breath normally for two breaths and now turn your focus to your back.

Take a deep breath, hold it for five seconds while tightening the muscles in your back. Then exhale slowly and relax your back muscles. Take two more breaths to relax. Take another deep breath. Then tighten the muscles in your back one more time while you hold your breath for five seconds. Exhale slowly as you relax your back muscles completely.

Take two normal breaths while you turn your attention to your neck and back.

Take a deep breath and hold it for five seconds while you tighten the muscles of your neck and back. Relax your muscles as you exhale slowly. Take two normal breaths to relax. Take another deep breath and again tighten the muscles of your back and neck for five seconds before relaxing your muscles again as you exhale.

Take two normal breaths and turn your focus to your hands and arms.

Take a deep breath and hold it for five seconds while making a tight fist and flexing your right forearm and biceps. Then exhale slowly as you relax your hand and arm. Take two normal breaths. Now take another deep breath and hold it for five seconds while making a fist and flexing your left forearm and biceps. Exhale slowly while relaxing your left arm and hand. Take two more breaths to relax. Take a deep breath and hold it for five seconds while you tighten both fists and flex both arms. Then exhale slowly as you relax your arms and open your hands feeling the tension release from the body.

Take two normal breaths as you begin to think shoulders.

Take a deep breath and hold it for five seconds as you roll your shoulders and then exhale slowly as you relax your shoulders. Take two more breaths to relax. Take another deep breath and hold it for five seconds as you roll your shoulders again. Exhale slowly and relax your shoulders. Notice the relaxation you feel reminds you of a good shoulder massage.

Take two normal breaths as you begin to focus on your entire body.

If you feel tension in any part of your body that distracts you from your general feeling of total relaxation, then focus on that muscle group and repeat the process.

Now that your muscles are relaxed from your head to your toes I want you to focus on your breathing. Take a deep breath, hold it for five seconds without tensing any muscles and as you exhale notice how completely relaxed and peaceful you feel. Take another deep breath, holding for only a second and then exhale again slowly.

Let your breathing gradually become more and more shallow and relaxed until your breathing is totally natural. Notice a wave of relaxation slowly flood though your entire body.

Enjoy this breathing and relaxation as long as you wish and when you decide to get up you will feel completely relaxed, refreshed and prepared to successfully handle whatever challenges you may face.

This exercise is strictly designed to help your archers develop their skill of progressive relaxation. By combining the use of Positive Affirmations (see below) in the final stages of the Progressive Relaxation exercise they can even enjoy an introduction to Self-Hypnosis which will open an entirely new area of exploration on their journey to the top.

This is JMU archer Brian Miles preparing himself mentally between shots at the 2019 U.S. National Outdoor Collegiate Championships.

31

The Mental Game – Mental Imagery

The wonderful television coverage that we enjoyed during the 2012 Olympic archery competition provided us an excellent opportunity to experience competition in a way never before possible. We were able to see, up close and personal, the struggles and triumphs of the world's greatest archers during the most stressful conditions imaginable.

Giving your team the mental game sales pitch I discussed in a previous chapter along with them having just seen the Olympic archery competition on TV should convince a number of your archers to approach you about learning more about the mental game. Which places you in the driver's seat so let's make sure you know where you're going.

Regardless of which mental tools the Olympic archers may have used during the Games and during preparation for the Games you can be sure that they had invested the time and energy to try these and others techniques to see which work best for them as they developed their personal mental game plan.

The Mental Game Tools
Focus/Concentration
Controlled Breathing
Progressive Relaxation
Mental Imagery
Positive Self-Talk
Positive Affirmations
Comfort Zones/Resetting Your Thermostat
Managing Conscious Thoughts – During the Shot

When introducing the mental game to your students you should start with something you feel comfortable talking about and something you feel they will easily identify with. Mental imagery is just what the doctor ordered. Everyone can remember shooting hoops in their backyard, pretending to be in a basketball game, counting down the final seconds and swishing a shot at the buzzer to win the game. That is the most basic use of mental imagery. In a matter of seconds you observed yourself in an imaginary sporting event, against an imaginary opponent, successfully performing a difficult task in a pressure packed situation. It was fun and you thought it served no earthly purpose except to entertain yourself but, in fact, each time you put yourself through that situation successfully, you actually improved your confidence that you could respond under pressure.

Now, if games we play in our mind with no purpose can have a positive impact, imagine what we can accomplish if we have a plan. To be candid with you, I use mental imagery to prepare myself for contract negotiations, public speaking, and even as a tournament director. One of the reasons I have enjoyed running so many successful archery tournaments over the years, including 40 or so national championship events, is the fact that I actually take the time to dissect the event into its various critical areas and try to visualize everything that could possibly go wrong and then visualize a successful response to each crisis imagined. If you can visualize the worst possible circumstance and then prepare for that scenario, no one will ever know what kind or disaster almost happened. They will only tell you later how smoothly things ran.

> **Dream It ... Visualize It ... Achieve It.**

I don't ever want my archers to go into a tournament without taking the same types of steps to prepare for their success. While I expect my more mature archers to eventually use mental imagery to imagine, challenge, and conquer their demons we will introduce them to mental imagery in a more "paint by numbers" style.

I have prepared a short script to help archers get the feel of mental imagery without having to reinvent the wheel.

Instructions I want you to sit down with the script in your hand, get in a relaxed position, close your eyes and take two or three deep breaths to relax yourself. Now open your eyes and read the script slowly. (Try this yourself.)

Mental Imagery Recurve
Please use this script as an example to write your own or simply change a few words to match your personal style and form and use it as one aid to help you

master your mental game.

A Script for Success

As I step up to the waiting line I can smell the fresh cut grass. I feel a light breeze on my face. I can hear the crowd . . . talking . . . and laughing . . . but I can also sense the tension among the other competitors.

I hear two whistle blasts as we are called to the shooting line.

As I take my place on the shooting line . . . I can hear the crowd noise start to subside.

I reach in my quiver . . . searching for Arrow #1 . . . there it is.

I draw the arrow out of my quiver . . . snap it on the string . . . and set it on the rest.

I carefully work my bow hand as high into the grip as I can . . . then I relax my hand down onto the grip as I curl the fingers on my bow hand.

I place my tab on the string with the string placed in the first joint of my fingers.

I now put a little tension on the string . . . drawing about an inch or two . . . checking to make sure everything feels right before raising the bow to the target.

I hear one whistle blast.

Without changing the draw tension . . . I raise the bow until the aperture is on the gold . . . where I hold about a second.

Then I proceed to full draw without taking my eye off the gold.

As I come to full draw . . . I get an anchor with the knuckle on my index finger making solid contact with my jaw, my kisser button on my tooth and the string against my nose. As I get to my anchor I glance down to make sure my clicker is on the point of my arrow.

Now my concentration shifts back to the gold. Since the breeze is light . . . I center my aperture on the X . . . as I transfer to back tension in preparation for my release.

The clicker goes off and my fingers instantly relax off the string and slide back along my neck. The bow jumps forward out of my hand but is caught securely by my finger sling. My bow arm stays in place as my followthrough lasts till well after the arrow has hit the

209

mark.

The arrow strikes the ten . . . just touching the X and vibrates there briefly as if waving back to me saying . . . "Hey, great shot!"

I take one deep calming breath as I prepare for my next shot.

Now, I pull Arrow #2 out of my quiver and load it onto the bow.

I set my grip just right and then put my fingers on the string.

Then I put a little pressure on the string . . . raise my bow to the target and hold for about a second.

Going to full draw . . . I set up strong . . . and draw to my anchor. The breeze has picked up a bit . . . so I calculate my aiming point to be the 8/9 line at 3 o'clock to compensate for the drift.

Using back tension, I pull through the clicker and finish the shot with a strong follow through.

The second arrow slides right down the shaft of the first arrow . . . in the ten just off the X.

I load Arrow #3 onto the bow and take another deep breath.

I realize it's my third shot so I make a point to review the game plan in my head before the shot. Stand Tall . . . Set Up Strong . . . and Be Aggressive!

And the third arrow slaps the first two loudly as it proudly announces it's arrival in the ten ring.

Ends like this make for an awfully short walk to the target! As compound archers can benefit from this same skill I have prepared a sample script for them as well.

Mental Imagery Compound

Please use this script as a sample to write your own or simply change a few words to match your personal style and form and use it as one aid to help you master your mental game.

A Script for Success

As I step up to the waiting line I can smell the fresh cut grass. I feel a light breeze on my face. I can hear the crowd . . . talking . . . and laughing . . . but I can also sense the tension among the other competitors.

I hear two whistle blasts as we are called to the shooting line.

As I take my place on the shooting line . . . I can hear the crowd noise start to subside.

I reach in my quiver . . . searching for Arrow #1 . . . there it is.

I draw the arrow out of my quiver . . . snap it on the string . . . and set it on the rest.

I carefully work my bow hand as high into the grip as I can . . . then I relax my hand down onto the grip as I curl the fingers on my bow hand.

I slip my release into the string loop and set the hook. Then I let my fingers settle into the finger grooves on the release.

I now put a little tension on the string . . . drawing it about an inch or two . . . checking to make sure everything feels right before raising the bow to the target.

I hear one whistle blast.

Without changing the draw tension . . . I raise the bow until the sight is on the gold . . . where I hold about a second. Then I proceed to full draw without taking my eye off the gold.

As I come to full draw . . . I get an anchor with the knuckle on my hand making solid contact with my jaw and the string against my nose. As I get to my anchor I make sure I've pulled my string to a solid position against the wall.

Now my concentration shifts back to the gold. Since the breeze is light . . . I center my scope around the X . . . with both centered in the peep . . . as I add back tension to squeeze off the release.

The release goes off and slides back along my neck. The bow jumps forward out of my hand but is caught securely by my finger sling. My bow arm stays in place as my followthrough lasts till well after the arrow has hit the mark.

The arrow strikes the ten . . . just touching the X and vibrates there briefly as if waving back to me saying . . . "Hey, great shot!"

I take one deep calming breath as I prepare for my next shot.

Now I pull Arrow #2 out of my quiver and load it onto the bow.

I set my grip just right and then attach my release on the D-loop.

Then I put a little pressure on the string . . . raise my bow to the target and hold for about a second.

Going to full draw . . . I set up strong . . . string against the wall. The breeze has picked up a bit . . . so I calculate my aiming point to be the 8/9 line at 3 o'clock to compensate for the drift.

Using back tension, I squeeze the release off and finish the shot with a strong follow through.

The second arrow slides right down the shaft of the first arrow . . . in the ten just off the X.

I load Arrow #3 onto the bow and take a deep breath.

I realize it's my third shot so I make a point to review the game plan in my head before the shot. Stand Tall . . . Set Up Strong . . . and Be Aggressive!

And the third arrow slaps the first two loudly as it proudly announces it's arrival in the ten ring.

Ends like this make for an awfully short walk to the target!

Summary

Have your archers try these sample scripts. Have them modify one to their particular shooting styles and equipment variations. Then give them a chance. First try to visualize yourself shooting from within your own body, seeing only what you can see with your own eyes. Then try visualizing your shots from a position on the waiting line where you are actually observing yourself shooting. This allows you to see you improve your stance, alignment, clearance, release, and followthrough.

Don't hesitate to combine the use of video along with mental imagery as it helps to bring a sense of reality into the images you visualize and help you to hone in on the desired improvements you wish to achieve.

This is just the beginning and you have your homework. There's no limit to what you can achieve. Dream It . . . Visualize It . . . Achieve It.

This is JMU archer Caroline McCracken staying positive at the 2019 U.S. National Outdoor Collegiate Championships.

32
The Mental Game –
Positive Self-Talk

You wouldn't beat up on your kids when they don't perform up to your standards, so why would you allow them to do it to themselves?

Next, I'm going to pull Positive Self-Talk out of our Mental Tool Bag to discuss another way to help your team members develop a stronger mental game both individually and as a team.

The Mental Game Tools
Focus/Concentration
Controlled Breathing
Progressive Relaxation
Mental Imagery
Positive Self-Talk
Positive Affirmations
Comfort Zones/Resetting Your Thermostat
Managing Conscious Thoughts – During the Shot

We concentrate so hard on making sure that we teach, coach, and guide our team in a positive manner that builds their confidence and self-image we sometimes don't see our work being unraveled right before our eyes. I realize there is a lot going on when you are with your team but I encourage you to listen closely to what is being said when they think you're not listening. You may be surprised by the negative and sometimes abusive language that you will hear being used by your team members when talking about themselves and others on the team.

They may not have learned this behavior from you but, believe it or not, your team has been and will continue to be influenced by other people in their lives. (I know, shocking isn't it.) Their parents, friends and previous coaches/teachers and others all make up the influence that has shaped who they are by the time you meet them. It's a lot to ask to try to replace the influences in their lives that you may find counterproductive to your goals. Just remember, that as you fight to reduce the negative impact of previous influences that are detrimental to the achievement of your goals you are also fighting the good fight that will provide an environment that will allow the healthy growth and development of each of your individual archers.

Create a Positive Environment

Leave the negative outside the door. Hang a sign, make an announcement and print it in your range guidelines and team rules. We do not have any time for negativity in the practice room or on the archery field. Gone is the sound of "You Suck" and "As long as you're going to shake like that would you mind making me a martini."

When every comment from the veterans on your team is supportive and encouraging to their younger teammates it is easy to get the ball rolling for everyone. You don't have to check your sense of humor at the door. You just have to make sure that you put a governor on the insults and be ever mindful of the fragile confidence and self-images that we are trying to nurture.

We don't throw our equipment, we don't curse on the line, and we don't talk or behave in a manner that disrupts other competitors. We don't give up, we don't give the impression we are giving up and we don't ruin the competitive experience for any of our competitors. We shoot our arrows, process the results, and make necessary adjustments to compete to the best of our ability right up to the final whistle.

What Is Positive Self-Talk?

Positive self-talk is a very valuable tool for many people, not only in competition but specifically in developing a healthier self-image.

If you've ever heard me screaming in the team round you will recall hearing positive encouraging statements such as "Strong Shot" rather than negative statements such as "Don't Pluck." Quite simply, in this case, I don't want to even suggest or imply the possibility of a counterproductive activity. Instead I want to encourage or reinforce a productive action.

The same goes for verbalized or non-verbalized self-talk. When you shoot a good arrow what do you say or think to yourself? You should reinforce your performance immediately to build up your self-confidence and eventually your self-image. Some people just give a simple nod, some pat themselves on the back of their head, others say things like "Ring the Bell" but the funniest I have heard is a friend of mine from Virginia Beach would always say "Bulls

Ear Cat Nip!" every time he shot a 10. Regardless of what your personality is, I encourage them to work something positive into their routine as a form of reinforcement.

More important, though, is that what you say to yourself when a shot does not go as planned. Lanny Bassham, author of "With Winning in Mind," would encourage you to say something like: "That's not like me" or "It's like me to shoot 10's." Lanny Bassham is a successful author and the creator of Mental Management Systems, a consulting firm in the area of mental management. I highly recommend his books, tapes, and courses to anyone wishing to develop their mental game (www.mentalmanagement.com).

Each competitor has their own personality, and self-talk that works for one will not necessarily work for another. What is important to understand here is that they should explore different techniques and find what works for them. What is the talk they need to have with themself that not only reinforces successful shots and behavior but also helps them deal with unsuccessful shots or behavior?

> **Remember, this is a simple game to play but hard to perfect.**

Whatever style of talk they choose, the goal is to deal with the bad shot quickly and flush it and the memory of it immediately and start the next shot full of confidence making sure that there is no hangover of sadness, gloom and doom, or negativity of any type. We shoot these arrows one at a time and each one of them deserves all the love and positive vibes we can give it. For them to continue their anger, sadness, or disappointment from arrow #1 to arrow #2 is counterproductive and just not fair to their arrows, their score and to themself. It's like punishing your second child for the actions of the first. You've got to be a better parent of each of your shots than that.

Knowledge and experience play a big part in being able to move on in a tournament. Think about it. When you shoot a bad shot. You want to accept it and move on, but I also find it much easier to accept it and move on once I figure out what happened to cause the bad shot. With 50+ years of archery experience, most of the time I know what the cause of the bad shot was before the arrow hits the target. And yes, I treat a poorly shot 10 with the same disdain as a poorly shot 7. It is best if you can identify where you went wrong before you move on to self-talk and preparation for the next shot. Part of positive self-talk is being honest with ourselves.

Example 1 If the arrow went low and you dropped your bow arm on the shot, it's appropriate to handle it by saying "That shot was not like me. I shoot with a strong followthrough" and then follow that with mental imagery watching yourself shooting a strong shot with a good followthrough. Then shoot the next shot the way you are supposed to. Reward that shot with more positive self-talk.

The proper use of self-talk provides an opportunity to strengthen your self-image with every shot you take. Take advantage of it.

Example 2 If you shoot what felt like a strong shot but notice that it drifted farther in the wind that you anticipated, it's appropriate to handle it by saying "That was a good shot and I am learning to read the wind better with every shot" and then follow that with mental imagery watching yourself read the flag, hold the sight off and shooting a strong shot into the ten ring. Then shoot the next shot and follow it with more positive self-talk.

Remember, this is a simple game to play but hard to perfect. By addressing our imperfections in this manner, we will come closer to perfect every day. We don't need to be perfect to win…we just need to strive for perfection with every shot we take. Winning will come as we continue to strive for perfection.

Use Your Journal

You have explained to your team the value of positive self-talk. You can develop exercises to teach your team how to change their self-talk from negative to positive and you can have your veterans and squad leaders serve as a support system to reinforce their efforts and provide help along the way. Now, I think it is time to get them to buy into the program to the level where they show they understand the value and make the investment of being responsible for their own development and personal success.

Have them get out their Archery Journals and start recording descriptions of their observations, successes and failures while using the positive self-talk we have been discussing in this chapter.

Change the Team Cheer

It's time to retire the old team cheer that the kids used to do half way through a tournament when things weren't going very well for something more consistent with our Positive Self-Talk.

Retire this one: "FIDO!" (Forget It . . . Drive On!)

And maybe replace it with: "POLKA!" (Practice is Over…Let's Kick Ass!)

Here JMU archer Daniel Suter and I are reviewing his positive affirmations.

33

The Mental Game –
Positive Affirmations

The process of coaching collegiate archers over a period of four years offers an opportunity to do more far more that just develop archery skills. You have the opportunity to guide their development as competitive archers, students, and even as human beings. With this in mind, I do take certain liberties when introducing my students to positive affirmations.

The Mental Game Tools
Focus/Concentration
Controlled Breathing
Progressive Relaxation
Mental Imagery
Positive Self-Talk
Positive Affirmations
Comfort Zones/Resetting Your Thermostat
Managing Conscious Thoughts – During the Shot

Positive affirmations are used by people throughout their lives to help guide themselves through many aspects of their personal development. I personally like how well they work with the use of the goals they set in their journey to become world class archers.

One of the things I promise my archers when we start up each year is that no matter what kind of hell I may be dealing with at work or in my personal life when I walk through the door to the archery room I will leave all those problems outside the door. After explaining this and displaying a helpful professional attitude I simply ask them to do me the same courtesy. Once establishing those ground rules I rarely have to remind them of our deal.

Having developed a positive environment in which to work with these

221

new archers it is only one more step to introduce them to the power of positive affirmations. We explain that developing a positive mindset is one of the most powerful life strategies there is and that by using visualizations and positive affirmations, it is possible to achieve whatever you want.

At this point, it is very helpful to have them put some thought into setting goals for themselves. Yes, I know, entire books have been written on just the process of setting goals and with as many things are going on in a college student's life the last thing they need is another homework assignment. That's why we are going to keep our goal setting simple and do it during a team practice.

Tell them that while you are interested in how many kids they plan to have, where they want to live, that they want to find a cure for cancer and that they want to retire at 45: those are not the goals we need them to focus on at this time. There are many approaches to beginning to have your kids think about goals but one simple approach I like to use is to hand out a form that allows them to clearly establish their own goals in a relatively painless manner.

On the facing page there is another example of our goal development form (*see also pages 186-7*).

CONFIDENTIAL - Personal Goals   Name _____

Date _____

Overall Academic & Life Goals

Academic Goal _____

(Do you hope to graduate with honors or do you hope for a certain GPA?)

Degree Goal _____

(What is your major? And do you plan to pursue an advanced degree?)

Career Goal _____

(What do you plan to be doing for a living in 20 years?)

Archery Goal _____

(What is your ultimate goal in archery?)

Collegiate Goals

Academic Goals by Year (Circle All that Apply)

1st Year GPA 2.0 2.5 3.0 Dean's List President's List Other _____

2nd Year GPA 2.0 2.5 3.0 Dean's List President's List Other _____

3rd Year GPA 2.0 2.5 3.0 Dean's List President's List Other _____

4th Year GPA 2.0 2.5 3.0 Dean's List President's List Other _____

Archery Goals by Year (Circle All that Apply)

1st Year Join Club Make Team All-East All-American Top 3 Nat'l Champ World Champ

2nd Year Join Club Make Team All-East All-American Top 3 Nat'l Champ World Champ

3rd Year Join Club Make Team All-East All-American Top 3 Nat'l Champ World Champ

4th Year Join Club Make Team All-East All-American Top 3 Nat'l Champ World Champ

The Reality

Describe briefly where you think you are right now with your shooting.

_____

_____

The Dream

Restate your ultimate goal in Archery from above.

_____

_____

The Offer

What are you willing to do to make your dream become a reality. (Circle Them)
Cardio Training Weight Training Mental Training Learn Tuning Practice in
Windy Conditions Practice in Rain/Sleet/Snow

Other _____

Now that we have gotten them to think seriously enough to reduce their goals to writing it is up to us to help them take the next step. Generally, while the next step can be introduced to the group it will take a one-on-one meeting with each of your team members to help them to both buy in to the concept and to help them develop their first set of affirmations.

First review the goals that they recorded for you earlier and, after reviewing those items, I encourage them to put some thought into what kind of person they want to be as an adult. Who do they admire most and what qualities they have that they would most like to adopt themselves. Then expand that list to include other personality traits and qualities that they admire in other people that they would most like to emulate.

Now I explain that a positive affirmation is one statement that when met brings you one step closer to achieving the goals, written or unwritten, that we have established for ourselves. Then I hand them another form and ask them to complete the exercise, developing at least one positive affirmation in each of the categories listed.

The categories I like to include on the list are:
1. Academics
2. Conditioning
3. Personal Growth
4. Archery—Team Spirit
5. Archery—Practice
6. Archery—Mental Training
7. Archery—Shooting Form
8. Archery—Competition

After they take a minute to look over the list, they generally give you one of those looks that can best be described as "A Deer in the Headlights". It is at that point that I introduce another form which includes sample affirmations that I have developed over the years.

Positive Affirmation Exercise
Samples for Life & Training

The sample affirmations below are just that. Samples for you to consider while developing your own affirmations. You are welcome to use any of them, as written, or modify them to suit your needs.

Academics

I attend all classes, stay current at all times, and pass all classes with high marks.

Conditioning

I work on weight training at least twice a week and aerobic training three times a week.

Personal Growth

I am slow to anger, quick to forgive, and stand in judgement of no man.
I practice random acts of kindness at least once a day.

Team Spirit

I encourage and assist teammates at every opportunity.
I display a positive attitude at all team activities.

Practice

I attend practice and work on skill development five days a week.
I arrive on time and warm up before practice every day.

Mental Training

I work on positive affirmations seven days a week.

Samples for Shooting Form
Stance

I am careful to set up in the same stance every time I go to the line.

Finger Placement

I place my fingers on the string deliberately, placing the string in the first joint of my fingers.

Grip

My bow hand is relaxed and located in the same place on every shot.

Pre-Draw

I always put every thing in alignment during my Pre-Draw.

Draw

I draw smoothly, without interruption, through the completion of my shot.
I use back tension to complete the execution of my shot.

Anchor

My anchor point is exactly the same on every shot.

Aim

I burn a hole in the X-ring with my eyes and surround the hole with my aperture.
I only focus on the center of the target.

Release

My fingers are relaxed and my release is smooth.
I am mentally focused and am always surprised by the release.

Followthrough

My followthrough is consistent and I am still aiming when the arrow hits the ten.

Samples for Competition
Timing

I am aggressive on every shot and the timing of my shot sequence is always the same.
I am comfortable shooting my three arrows in 45 seconds.

Mental

I am comfortable shooting in front of spectators.
I am confident and relaxed when shooting in competition.
I am confident and relaxed when shooting in a major competition.
As a competitor I thrive on pressure.
I perform at my best when the competition is greatest.
I perform at my best in major competitions.

Combos

I'm relaxed and confident and shooting aggressively.
I feel strong and confident and my release is good.
I stand tall, set up strong, and shoot aggressively.

Once they have developed their own affirmations, have them write them on 3x5 cards. Then have them keep them where they will be able to read them three to five times a day. The purpose for some is to serve as a reminder of something they need to do, others to help them actually develop a new skill or mindset, and still others to keep them mindful of the person they want to become. Once they have gained control of one of the topics addressed by one of the 3x5 cards they should simply remove it from the rotation and upgrade to another topic, keeping their affirmations current and relevant at all times.

There is nothing easy about developing a better mental game. Archers have resisted working in this area more than any other aspect of their game. That's why it is particularly satisfying when you work with the one in a thousand who actually gets it and you get to see them succeed on the most stressful of all stages. Victory really can be theirs . . . but they have to believe they are worthy.

JMU archer John Haskens and I sit down to help him "Adjust His Thermostat."

34

The Mental Game – Comfort Zones/Thermostat Resetting

This chapter is aimed at those of you who live indoors. Most people who live indoors can thank Central Heating and Air Conditioning for maintaining the temperature of their house within a comfortable range. This range from your lowest acceptable temperature to your highest acceptable temperature is referred to as your Comfort Zone.

The Mental Game Tools
Focus/Concentration
Controlled Breathing
Progressive Relaxation
Mental Imagery
Positive Self-Talk
Positive Affirmations
Comfort Zones/Resetting Your Thermostat
Managing Conscious Thoughts – During the Shot

What's amazing is that comfort zones not only exist in the area of home climate control but are also a very real item to deal with in the world of competitive archery. I know, you think I've lost my mind again. But I'll bet you a dollar to a donut that all archers who have shot much competitive archery have found themselves in a competition in which they were shooting lights out when they started the event, shooting way above their average, but as the round continued they found themselves experiencing some of the most creative ways to lose points, allowing them to finish the competition without that new personal best they were on pace for. Instead they ended up within a few points of their average score. That's sad, but to balance it out, they have also probably experienced just the opposite. Where they couldn't seem to get warmed up at first but as time went on they got on a streak and by the end of the round they finished up . . . wait for it . . . within a few points of their average.

And not only has this happened to them, but it has happened to you.

No, I do not have the power to read your mind as you are reading this chapter. It's just that the vast majority of experienced archers who I have coached over the past 30 years or so have confessed that they have experienced this same phenomenon. Isn't the mind a fun thing to have to playing tricks on us when we are working so hard every day to improve our skills? Many times I think we could all be better archers if we had a lobotomy. I must confess that much of the mental game that we try to develop is not geared toward having the mind take a more active role, but having it take a less active role.

In the area of comfort zones, we as coaches welcome the mind's involve-

Robin Hood				End	Running		Analysis		
End	1	2	3	Score	Score		Best Quarter	Best Consec 5	
1	10	10	9	29	29				
2	10	9	7	26	55				
3	10	9	9	28	83				
4	10	9	9	28	111				
5	8	8	8	24	135		1	135	
6	10	9	8	27	162				
7	9	7	6	22	184				
8	9	9	8	26	210				
9	9	9	8	26	236				
10	10	9	8	27	263		2	128	
11	10	9	8	27	290				
12	9	9	7	25	315				
13	10	8	3	21	336				
14	9	8	5	22	358				
15	10	10	9	29	387		3	124	X	29
16	10	9	9	28	415				X	28
17	10	10	8	28	443				X	28
18	9	8	8	25	468				X	25
19	10	9	9	28	496				X	28	138
20	9	8	8	25	521		4	134	
Totals: 60 Arrows					521		540		552

Analysis					
By End	10	9	8		
	9	7	10	26	547
By Arrow	9	9	9		
	1	7	26	34	555

This archer recently shot a personal best of 564 and hopes to utilize these and other training techniques to continue his development towards his goal of making the Olympic Team.

ment and actually use it to improve our student's results. Just as the Central Heating and Air Conditioning in your home has a thermostat that controls the climate in your house, we also have thermostats in our minds. It has been set over time by living through our historical performances and our acceptance of these performances. For the purpose of keeping life simple in this chapter we will be referring to indoor scores as related to a 60 arrow Indoor FITA I Round (20 ends of three arrows, 10-9-etc. scoring, at 18 m distance). If you have shot an average of 540 over the past year or two the thermostat in your mind is satisfied that you are a 540 shooter. Where the rub comes in is how do you ever become a 560 or 570 shooter if the thermostat in your mind is satisfied that you are a 540 shooter. Just like with the temperature at home the only way to make the heat or the scores go up is to change the thermostat.

Hold it . . . before you make yourself miserable in your own home trying to improve your scores by cranking up the thermostat, let me explain how I like to do it with my archers.

Every scorecard, no matter how horrible the score, is a treasure chest of opportunities for the motivation of your archers. The idea is not to point out, relive, or dwell on the errors that were made. The idea is to analyze their performance in a way that actually displays for them, in a logical manner, a revised view of their performance that establishes a new level of expectation that they can rationalize in their own mind. This, in effect, serves to raise their mental thermostat, changing their comfort zone.

I have included within this chapter a re-creation of an actual scorecard from the 2012 US Indoor Archery Championship (*see opposite page*).

When I am analyzing scorecards for the purpose of raising thermostats and changing comfort zones I use one or more of the following techniques.

1. **Best Quarter**

   Show the archer the ends she shot in her best quarter and ask her if there is any reason she shouldn't be able to maintain that pace for the entire round. Then, when she agrees that that is a reasonable expectation, take the archer's best quarter and multiply by 4 to create a revised score, a score that represents what she will shoot with that level of performance.

2. **Best Consecutive Five Ends**

   If the archer you are reviewing really struggled putting a full quarter together then check to see if what their best consecutive five ends are. Then ask him if there is any reason he shouldn't be able to maintain that pace for a whole round. Then, when he agrees that that is reasonable, then multiply that score times four to create a revised score.

3. **Each End**

   Another way of analyzing the scorecard that may yield a more satisfactory result is to establish the archer's lowest acceptable end score. You both have to agree on this end. For example, the archer you are working with should always hold red and shoots gold most of the time. You may agree on an end of 10, 9, 8 as the lowest acceptable end. In this case, with a black ink pen, circle each first arrow that's not a 10, each second arrow that is below a 9, and each third arrow that is lower than an 8. Then add up the points that the archer missed and add that to the total her total score to come up with a revised score.

4. **Each Arrow**

One more way of analyzing the scorecard is to simply establish, with your archer, a lowest acceptable arrow score. This will show clearly the impact that flyers can have on the outcome and total score. With a red ink pen circle every arrow that is below that score. Add the total difference in points of all those arrows and then add that sum to his total score to come up with the revised score.

The best thing about these analysis techniques is that, when used in a responsible manner, they work. What I mean by this is that you need to know the skill level and dedication of the archer you are analyzing and try to balance your desire to motivate him with a practical attempt at helping him set realistic expectations. It should be obvious that the archers you work with in college are not stupid.

If you are working with an archer who just shot a 350 in his first tournament, it is not likely that he will buy into a motivational analysis that attempts to say that since he shot one 10 that day that there is no reason he shouldn't be able to do that on every shot and try to sell him on the expectation of shooting a 600 in his next round of competition. Instead, you need to have an honest private conversation with each of your archers allowing a comfortable but serious discussion where you have the opportunity to help them buy into the concept. By explaining that nothing comes easy and if they want to live up to the potential that they have shown they will need work hard on the program you have put together for them.

There are also other things that you can learn from closely reviewing scorecards. I will often times make certain observations during the scorecard analysis. Take a look at the quarter totals and after a brief review don't hesitate to share your learned observations. For example:

1. **If an archer shoots 125, 135, 140, then 135**

Ask the archer if they were nervous at the start or if they just didn't have a good sight setting. This normally leads to an interesting conversation that will end up with you outlining start up drills you want him to work on that gets him used to dealing with pressure and expectations right out of the box. You may have him start practice with only a single 3-arrow practice end followed by scoring five 3-arrow ends.

2. **If an archer shoots 140, 130, 135, then 140**

   Tell the archer how proud you are of the way they started and even the way they finished. Then, ask the archer if they lost their focus in the middle of the round. This again will lead to an interesting conversation with the result being you trying to help him hone his shot routine, for example to build in a cleansing breath which leads to a fresh approach to concentration on each arrow of every end.

3. **If an archer shoots 130, 125, 115, then 110**

   Ask the archer if he ran out of gas or if he was simply losing his eyesight. Normally he will be honest and admit he has not been at practice as much as he had planned to but he will agree to follow your recommendation and work hard to build up his arrow count before the next competition.

These are just some of the many things you can learn from looking closely at your archers' scorecards. Each card is a gold mine and should be reviewed as soon after a competition as possible because you don't want a kid to go around thinking they are a 520 shooter when you know you can convince them they are a 540 shooter. Do your kids a favor and yourself a favor by trying this. The success of your team just might be one of the dividends.

This an old photo of me managing my conscious thoughts during a pre-draw.

35

The Mental Game – Managing Conscious Thoughts

Once you have taught your team about the first eight tools in developing their mental game it is time to introduce them to Managing Conscious Thought throughout the shot process. They can understand all of the other tools or steps in their mental game plan but until they grasp this tool they will be at the mercy of their subconscious mind during their most vulnerable times . . . in competition.

The Mental Game Tools
Focus/Concentration
Controlled Breathing
Progressive Relaxation
Mental Imagery
Positive Self-Talk
Positive Affirmations
Comfort Zones/Resetting Your Thermostat
Managing Conscious Thoughts – During the Shot

As you discuss the topic of managing conscious thought with your team it is important to be mindful that your kids, like mine, are going to be at various levels of development and you want them to understand what to do with the concept at their particular level. While some of your team members will probably be ready, and in fact, need to master this tool to advance their competitiveness, others on your team may just now be learning the basics and may get a greater return on time invested by practicing basic form at this stage in their development. For that reason, I would like to make a brief statement to clear up how to manage conscious thought throughout their development as tournament archers.

Nothing changes more during an archer's journey from Novice to Champion than the job description your conscious mind is responsible for.

Generally speaking, your brain is a relatively useful and cooperative piece of equipment that comes standard with nearly every human body. We use them for everything and we get used to counting on them in all situations. So why do I recommend you warn your kids not to trust their brains when it comes to the shot process in competition?

Like fair weather friends, your brain can be trusted until it is needed. It's as simple as that. What makes me say that? Over 50 years of experience in the

Level	Activity	Conscious Thoughts
Novice	Learning to shoot	Focus on learning and mimicking each step as taught.
New Archer	Practice	Focus specifically on the skill you are working on.
Archer	Practice	Focus first on perfecting your shot and then on developing facilitation and timing allowing a series of related steps to become a single mindless activity through thousands of practice shots.
Intermediate	Practice Scoring	Low stress scoring does not match the intensity of competition but will allow you to practice not only shooting for score but the mental game you plan to use in competition. Give yourself a lobotomy. Once you have developed your shooting form, perfected your shot and fine tuned your equipment . . .your mind is your greatest risk to your success . . . and it must be controlled.

Intermediate	Competition	If you don't have a game plan for controlling your mind . . . your mind will control your game. The skill level you have attained and the preparations you have made determine the peak performance you can deliver. Your mind's control of your performance will determine the success you achieve. Will it allow you to perform at 100% of your potential or maybe just 80%? You decide if you want to just let it happen . . . or if you want to take control of your own destiny by developing and implementing your mental game
Advanced	Competition	Use the mental game plan you have developed through practice and competition. Control the subconscious decay of your shot process by using your conscious mind . . . by deciding on and using planned conscious thought to block unplanned thought processes from your subconscious mind. This will leave your subconscious mind to facilitate your shot process.

field of archery competition as a competitor and as a coach has presented a plethora of examples.

One example that comes to mind is a kid who came to JMU as a shooter with a lot of experience in small tournaments and even worked in a pro shop in the off season. He had great form, a positive attitude, worked harder than anyone else on the team and even helped teach new archers. But archery was so important to him that when a tournament came up he couldn't deal with the pressure and fell apart right from the first whistle. Half way through the tournament he would be so far off the pace he calmed down and shot like a champ. I could see that once he was out of the running and he didn't care anymore, there was no more pressure and he could shoot the way he knew how to shoot. I failed him in that I was never able get him to buy into the mental game and as a result he never won an event his entire time with the team. I'm thankful that over the years I've always had good kids and most of the time they were willing to listen. Maybe I just didn't catch him early enough.

When coaching your kids and trying to determine when to introduce various aspects of the mental game it is important to understand where they are as competitors. I am sorry to say that it has less to do with their individual skill levels than it does with the expectations that they have placed upon themselves. Not to try and sound too much like Yogi Berra, the great Yankee Baseball Player, but "You don't really need to control your conscious thought until you need to control your conscious thought."

This is a part of the game that nobody needs until they need it. Your kids won't be interested in working on this because you say it is important. You can tell your kids not to touch the hot stove, but it is not a wise or important instruction until they touch the hot stove and get burned themselves. Herein lies your problem as their coach. You can introduce the concept of controlling conscious thought anytime during their development but until they touch the hot stove for themselves it will have no place in their world.

> **"**
> *If you don't have a game plan for controlling your mind . . . your mind will control your game.*
> **"**

Some archers may go through their entire archery career without ever experiencing this disconnect while some barely get started. Why is that? When do your expectations cause your brain to choke the performance out of you? The vast majority of competitors have to have earned some level of success in the sport before they become vulnerable. When you have a kid who has been the most naturally gifted, is the fastest learner on your team, and he wins his first tournament or title you have to immediately go on alert to his vulnerability and consider seriously the thought of introducing him to the concept of managing conscious thought.

Your brain is one of the most active and definitely the most creative organs in the body. If you don't plan a dialogue for your conscious mind it will come up with one of its own. For example:

"This tournament is the last USAT Ranking Event. If I don't finish in the top three here I won't have a chance of making the team."

"This has been a tough year so far. If I don't win this one, I'll probably lose all my sponsors for next year."

"OMG! I can only drop one more point over the next four ends if I'm going to finish with a 580."

"I won my first tournament last weekend. If I don't win today everybody will think I was just lucky."

"I can't hit the broad side of a barn today! If I don't pick it up even that goof ball is going to beat me."

"Dad spent all this money on my new bow. If I don't do better than last time he's going to think I'm not really trying."

"I've got to shoot better. The whole team is counting on me."

Remember the scene in "Back to the Future" when Michael J. Fox's character, Marty McFly, is looking at a picture of his family where he and his siblings slowly disappear. I contend that sometimes it's like your kids choose to visualize themselves on the top of the podium and as they continue to shoot beneath their expectations their position slowly changes until they disappear from the podium entirely.

This is the pressure these kids can put on themselves purely from their own self-imposed expectations regardless if they are influenced by internal or external sources.

So what can we do to help our kids manage their conscious thoughts during the shot process? Since your mind is going to think about something, no matter how counterproductive it might be, we need to have them put positive productive thoughts in their minds throughout every second of the shot process.

Your archers have to buy into whatever the thought is that will be implanted into their shot process but I will share with you what I use myself.

When I go to the line I take my stance, I make myself aware of existing conditions, and when the whistle blows I think "Stand Tall, Set Up Strong and Be Aggressive." Once I hit my anchor I start with "One, Two, Three" and I release. Since I admit that I combine control of my conscious mind with timing control, I need you to understand that while my goal is to perform that in three seconds or less the time can vary greatly as long as you release during the third count. Later in the season, when my timing is actually working for me I like to substitute "Dead, Solid, Perfect" in place of One, Two, Three.

When Daniel Suter won the World Championships in 2012 he had substituted O, S, N in place of the 1, 2, 3 but it seemed to work just fine. I'm sure Daniel would be happy to explain the meaning to anyone who asks. The point is that if you put something into your conscious mind . . . the demons can't get in. You can't think of two things at a time. What about the shot process? The shot process is handled completely by your subconscious mind. What do you think the tens of thousands of practice shots were for in the past year? That was to develop muscle memory and the facilitation of the shot. Your subconscious mind can get the tens if you can just keep the demons in your conscious mind from stealing them.

Try this out and let me know what winning positive thoughts you use to block the demons. And, if it works for you, teach it, teach it to your students.

This is me stepping off the line at the 1973 USIAC's with the national championship title and new national records. Doing something like this requires a complete mental game now more than ever because your competitors sure as heck will have one.

36

The Mental Game – Putting it All Together

Teaching your team about the mental game is not over once you have introduced them to all the tools listed below. Somehow you have to get them to understand how it all fits together to help them develop their own mental game.

The Mental Game Tools
Focus/Concentration
Controlled Breathing
Progressive Relaxation
Mental Imagery
Positive Self-Talk
Positive Affirmations
Comfort Zones/Resetting Your Thermostat
Managing Conscious Thought – During the Shot
. . . all together now!

Let's be honest with ourselves. Most of the kids we introduce these concepts to get lost in the shuffle. Either because they aren't committed enough to devote the necessary time and energy to work on one more aspect of their game or they're just not ready to understand the concepts. Either way, you're gambling when you bare your soul enough to share the concept of the mental game with them in the first place. So when you identify the small percentage of your students who "get it" and are ready to make the personal investment required to dedicate themselves to become "complete" competitors you have truly struck gold.

When you have introduced them to these techniques and they have had an opportunity to work through some of the exercises they will try implementing some of them. Once they have done this I think they will finally have enough of a point of reference for each of the tools introduced to allow you to show them how they all fit together. Let's review. . . .

Mental Training Tools

Focus/Concentration They learned to turn their concentration on and off like a light switch giving them the ability to fix their focus on one thing to the exclusion of all else.

Controlled Breathing They learned how to breathe between shots to reduce their heart rate and how to breathe during the shot to reduce fatigue and create the greatest stability.

Progressive Relaxation They learned how to relax specific muscle groups or their entire body, slow down everything around them, and take control of their game. With further development of this tool they will be able to improve relaxation, reduce stress, and even learn the skill of self-hypnosis.

Mental Imagery They learned how to improve their shooting technique, specific skills, and timing without even picking up our bow. We developed a tool that they could use to visualize difficult conditions and circumstances and appropriate successful responses to them.

Positive Self-Talk They learned how to develop a positive self-image by replacing counterproductive self-talk that punishes and causes them to dwell on negative results with positive language meant to allow them to move positively to the next shot.

Positive Affirmations They learned to work on their areas of weakness by developing positive affirmations that make a positive statement that they repeat several times a day to keep them focused on the positive development they are trying to achieve in these chosen areas of focus. They should not hesitate to add positive motivational quotes to their personalized positive affirmations in an effort to keep the sky blue and the impact positive.

Comfort Zones They learned that we all develop performance levels that they are comfortable with and their mind can make it very difficult to perform to a level far above or below this self-imposed zone.

Resetting Your Thermostat They learned specific techniques to increase the upper limits of their self-imposed comfort zone.

Managing Conscious Thoughts They learned how to use their conscious mind to control the subconscious decay of their shot process, one of the more dangerous enemies of elite performance.

This is an oversimplification of each of the mental skills we have addressed but it is important to do a brief review prior to moving on to the topic of how and when to use them. I thought that possibly the best way to explain how to put it all together is to introduce my mental game timeline.

When	What
Starting Now	*Develop Your Mental Game* Include all skills listed above.
Before a Tourney	*Progressive Relaxation* Use this opportunity to relax, reduce your heart rate and gain your composure prior to the competition.
	Mental Imagery Take the time to practice a few perfect shots in the actual venue to prepare yourself and build confidence prior to the whistle.
	Repeat Positive Affirmations Saying or reading your positive affirmations prior to the competition just reinforces the positive development you expect from yourself during the event.
Prior to the Shot	*Use Controlled Breathing* Controlled breathing will allow you to manage your heart rate, maintain your composure while you wait for the action to begin.
	Mental Imagery Take one more perfect shot to improve your confidence and timing while you wait for the whistle to start the end.
During the Shot	*Continue Controlling Your Breathing* Controlled breathing during the shot will assure you that your blood will be carrying enough oxygen to maintain your focus and stability through the completion of the shot.
	Focus/Concentration Turn your focus to the task at hand, the ten ring, while blocking out all distractions and other activities that do not contribute to accomplishing your goals.
	Manage Your Conscious Thoughts Use your planned conscious thought to block unplanned thought processes from your subconscious mind, freeing your subconscious mind to facilitate your shot process.
Between Shots	*Continue your Controlled Breathing* Take at least one deep breath between shots to replenish oxygen in the blood, to relax yourself and to reduce your heart rate.
	Practice Positive Self-Talk Find the positive and reinforce that feeling. If your shot fell short of your goal find what you did right, reinforce that and encourage yourself with positive thoughts or words. If your shot hit the mark reward yourself with positive thoughts or comments.

Between Shots (con't)	*Mental Imagery* There is no better mental implant than watching yourself shoot a perfect ten, so if that is what you shot…just relax and move on to the next shot. If not, visualize yourself shooting one perfect shot under the exact conditions you are currently experiencing . . . then move on to the next shot.
After the End	*Practice Positive Self-Talk* Use your thoughts or words to encourage, reinforce and reward yourself in a constant effort to grow your confidence and self-image knowing that this is a long term goal and you will either be your own best ally…or your own worst enemy.
	Repeat Positive Affirmations One way to regain your focus on the improvements that you are trying to make is to take a moment to review your positive affirmations. In the heat of the battle it is easy to get caught up in the pressure of the tournament and lose track of the very reason you are shooting this event… which is to improve and work yourself closer to your personal goals.
After the Tourney	*Reset Your Thermostat* Yes, I want you to take your scorecard and perform the analysis we discussed in our chapter on Resetting Your Thermostat. One method is to break it down by quarter to determine whether your lost more points due to stamina, nerves or loss of focus. Then see what your score would be if you shot the whole tournament like you shot your best quarter. Now, that is the score I want you to identify with. Forget the total score on your card. That's the old you and since we are eliminating the old errors we will accept the adjusted score as the archer we are now.
	Revise Your Positive Affirmations After each event, I suggest you review your positive affirmations and determine which one or ones are no longer needed and what new positive affirmation(s) you may need to add in their place. You are evolving as an archer and it is important to keep your positive affirmations current and meaningful in your development as a champion.

Mental Game Timeline

You can now introduce this complete program to your archers in preparation for their climb to the top of the podium. Whatever podium they hope to climb, unlike changes in equipment or form, there is no risk and their chances to reach it will only increase with the time they spend developing these skills.

Like every other tool you have in your box as a coach, if this one is not used properly it will not provide the desired results. No coach can inspire all of their students to buy into a concept and devote the time and energy necessary to succeed, but I can say with confidence that nothing included in my "Positive Approach to Mental Training" is counterproductive to a serious archer's growth and development.

Most of your students are willing to pay hundreds if not thousands of dollars to get the latest bobble or doodad designed to give them five more points. Here, they have the opportunity to remove the ceiling on their own self-imposed limitations for the small price of zero dollars. What it costs is much more valuable … it is their time and effort in an area that remains unexplored by many unsuccessful competitors on their road to mediocrity.

I challenge you and your students to …

Take a Chance,
Invest Time and Effort in Yourself, and Just Maybe
Become a Champion.

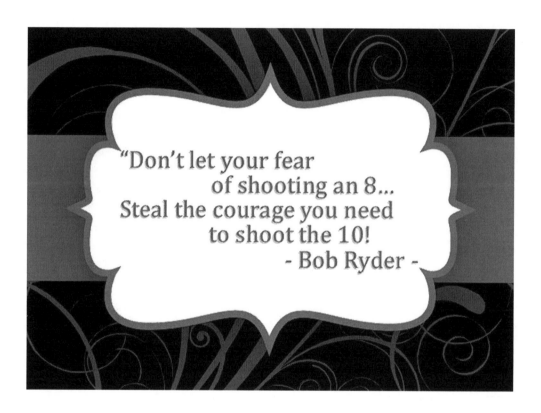

37

The Mental Game – Quiver Wisdom

Coaching a team presents some interesting differences from coaching individuals especially as you prepare for a major competition. You have a full-time job keeping just one or two kids heads from exploding at a special event they have been preparing for. When the number of kids you are coaching at the event jumps to 12, or in my case 30 or so with the JMU Archery Team, you look for ways to share some guidance more widely.

One way to expand the wisdom you hope to provide is through the use of a self-help guide. You have already taught your team the Tools of the Mental Game and helped them to understand how it all fits together. But sometimes, in a major competition they seem to find themselves all alone in the ocean, just looking for something to hang on to . . . in the hope of keeping them afloat until they are safe or help arrives. (That's you.)

The wisdom that you build into your self-help guide does not have to be strictly limited to archery. You should, where possible, keep in mind that these kids are still finding themselves and will benefit from more general inspiration which can be well suited to life in general as opposed to just archery.

Encourage your students to share their favorite quotes with you as you continue to build a pool of positive inspiration and wisdom, then provide them in whatever format or distribution system that suits your particular style.

What follows is a sampling of some of the quotes I have compiled for this purpose. We'll simply title it Quiver Wisdom.

Quiver Wisdom—Getting Started

It is never too late to be what you might have been.
George Eliot

Bob Ryder

Your talent is God's gift to you. What you do with it is your gift back to God.
Leo Buscaglia

The future depends on what we do in the present.
Mahatma Gandhi

You don't have to be the best to start, but you have to start to be the best.
Anonymous

Believe you can and you're halfway there.
Theodore Roosevelt

Quiver Wisdom—Goals

People with goals succeed . . . because they know where they're going.
Earl Nightingale

The quality of an individual is reflected in the standards
they set for themselves.
Ray Kroc

The will to win, the desire to succeed, the urge to reach your full potential . .
. these are the keys that will unlock the door to personal excellence.
Confucius

Accomplishing a goal is not as important . . . as the person you become
accomplishing it.
Anonymous

Shoot for the moon. Even if you miss, you'll land among the stars.
Les Brown

You must begin to think of yourself as becoming the person you want to be.
David Viscott

There isn't a person anywhere who isn't capable of doing more than he
thinks he can.
Henry Ford

Limitations live only in our minds. But if we use our imaginations . . . our possibilities become limitless.
Jamie Paolinetti

Behold the turtle. He only makes progress when he sticks his neck out.
James Bryant Conant

All our dreams can come true . . . if we have the courage to pursue them.
Walt Disney

The price for a small dream and a big dream is the same . . . it is one life, and it's yours.
Dave Tweely

Dream your dreams with open eyes and make them come true.
T.E. Lawrence

Quiver Wisdom—Training

The difference between a successful person and others is not a lack of strength, not a lack of knowledge . . . but rather a lack of will.
Vince Lombardi

I've always believed that if you put in the work, the results will come.
Michael Jordan

I hated every minute of training, but I said: 'Don't quit. Suffer now and live the rest of your life as a champion.'
Muhammad Ali

By failing to prepare you are preparing to fail.
Benjamin Franklin

You must pay the price if you wish to secure the blessings.
Andrew Jackson

I will prepare . . . and some day my chance will come.
Abraham Lincoln

There are no gains without pains.
Ben Franklin

The truth of the matter is that you always know the right thing to do. The hard part is doing it.
General H. Norman Schwarzkopf

Desire is the key to motivation, but it's the determination and commitment to an unrelenting pursuit of your goal – a commitment to excellence – that will enable you to attain the success you seek.
Mario Andretti

The greatest barriers in our pursuit of excellence are psychological barriers that we impose on ourselves, sometimes unknowingly.
Terry Orlick

The harder you work, the harder it is to surrender.
Vince Lombardi

Quiver Wisdom—Practice

Don't practice till you get it right . . . practice until you can't get it wrong.
Anonymous

Perfection is not attainable, but if we chase perfection . . .
we can catch excellence.
Vince Lombardi

Always do your best. What you plant now, you will harvest later.
Og Mandino

Do not let what you cannot do interfere with what you can do.
John Wooden

For the things we have to learn before we can do them,
we learn by doing them
Aristotle

Always do more than is required of you.
George S. Patton

The only way you should be able to tell it is practice . . . is by what you are wearing.
Anonymous

Everything should be made as simple as possible, but not simpler
Albert Einstein

I do the very best I know how, the very best I can, and I mean to keep doing so until the end.
Abraham Lincoln

Whatever is worth doing at all is worth doing well.
Lord Chesterfield

We are what we repeatedly do. Excellence, therefore, is not an act but a habit.
Aristotle

Knowing is not enough;
We must apply.
Willing is not enough;
We must do.
Goethe

I'm a great believer in luck, and I find the harder I work, the more I have of it.
Thomas Jefferson

Don't ask for the task to be easy, ask for it to be worth it.
Jim Rohn

The only place you'll find success before work is in the dictionary.
Vince Lombardi

Our greatest weakness lies in giving up. The most certain way to succeed is always to try just one more time.
Thomas A. Edison

No one can motivate you, until you motivate yourself.
Neeru

Bob Ryder

Quiver Wisdom—For the Day of Competition

To give anything less than your best, is to sacrifice the gift.
Steve Prefontaine

Look in the mirror, that's your competition.
Unknown

Don't let your fear of shooting an eight,
steal the courage you need to shoot the ten!
Bob Ryder

Whether you think you can, or think you can't, you're right.
Henry Ford

Nothing great was ever achieved without enthusiasm.
Ralph Waldo Emerson

The quality of a person's life is in direct proportion to their commitment to
excellence, regardless of their chosen field of endeavor.
Vince Lombardi

This is my day of opportunity. I will not waste it.
Anonymous

Quiver Wisdom—When Being Tentative on your Shot

Your Attention Please!
No one is coming to save you.
Finish the damned shot!
Bob Ryder

Quiver Wisdom—Bad Arrows

Forget past mistakes. Forget failures. Forget everything except what you're
going to do now and do it.
William Durant

Never let the fear of striking out get in your way.
Babe Ruth

Don't ruin your next arrow by worrying about your last one.
Let it go!
Bob Ryder

Quiver Wisdom—Bad Ends

Don't get your knickers in a knot. Nothing is solved and
it just makes you walk funny.
Kathryn Carpenter

Quiver Wisdom—Feeling Stress

Control your emotion or it will control you.
Samurai Maxim

May your choices reflect your hopes, not your fears.
Nelson Mandela

Quiver Wisdom—When Trailing the Competition

In a calm sea, every man is a pilot. Strength is proven in adversity.
English Proverb

Never, never, never give up.
Winston Churchill

Quiver Wisdom—When Feeling Low

Half-heartedness never won a battle.
William McKinley

A river cuts through rock, not because of its power, but it's persistence
Anonymous

When you are required to exhibit strength, it comes.
Joseph Campbell

When you come to the end of your rope, tie a knot and hang on.
Franklin D. Roosevelt

Be miserable. Or motivate yourself. Whatever has to be done,
it's always your choice.
Wayne Dyer

If you could kick the person in the pants responsible for most of
your trouble, you wouldn't sit for a month.
Theodore Roosevelt

Quiver Wisdom—After Winning

Be humble and gracious in victory. The kindness you show will be returned.
Bob Ryder

Quiver Wisdom—After Losing

Don't judge each day by the harvest you reap,
but by the seeds that you plant.
Robert Louis Stevenson

A successful person never loses, they either Win or Learn.
John Calipari

You may have to fight a battle more than once to win it.
Margaret Thatcher

Experience is not what happens to a man. It is what a man does
with what happens to him.
Aldous Huxley

If a man has done his best, what else is there?
George S. Patton

No one can make you feel inferior without your consent.
Eleanor Roosevelt.

When you fall, stand tall and come back for more.
Tupac Shakur

Winners never quit, and quitters never win.
Vince Lombardi

Our greatest glory is not in never failing
but in rising up every time we fail.
Ralph Waldo Emerson

The ultimate victory in competition is derived from the inner satisfaction of
knowing that you have done your best and that you have gotten the most
out of what you had to give.
Howard Cosell

Evaluate, improve, adjust. In these continual actions are the seeds of success.
Anonymous

Quiver Wisdom—Positive Affirmations

Stand tall, set up strong, and be aggressive.
Bob Ryder

It's the repetition of affirmations that leads to belief. And once that belief
becomes a deep conviction, things begin to happen.
Muhammad Ali

Quiver Wisdom—When In Need of Inspiration

What lies behind us and what lies before us, are tiny matters
compared to what lies within us.
Ralph Waldo Emerson

When everything seems to be going against you, remember that the airplane
takes off against the wind, not with it.
Henry Ford

Strength does not come from physical capacity. It comes from an
indomitable will.
Mahatma Gandhi

It is amazing what can be accomplished, when you don't care who gets the
credit.
John Wooden

In the middle of difficulty lies opportunity
Albert Einstein

When I was a young man I observed that nine out of the ten things I did were failures. Not wanting to be a failure, I did ten times more work.
George Bernard Shaw

Somedays you just have to create your own sunshine.
Anonymous

Quiver Wisdom—When Exhausted

Nobody ever drowned in sweat.
Steve Prefontaine

All that's not given . . . is lost.
Dominique Lapierre

Quiver Wisdom—Equipment Failures

Do what you can . . . with what you have . . . where you are.
Theodore Roosevelt

Quiver Wisdom—When Feeling Like the Underdog

Everybody pulls for David, nobody roots for Goliath.
Wilt Chamberlain

I have learned to use the word impossible with the greatest caution.
Werner von Braun

Obviously, you can assemble the quotes you use in any order using any categories that seem appropriate for your organization and use. Many of the quotes that you find inspiring may fit several different categories. Please let me know if you have quotes you think I might be able to use. I would appreciate any input or feedback you wish to share.

This is my coaching padfolio. Yes, coaches need to keep journals
just as much as archers need to.

38
The Mental Game – Keeping an Archery Journal

Did you ever have a really unpleasant experience that you didn't want to repeat. If so, while you want mercifully to forget that experience ever happened, you need to remember it in some way to keep it from happening again. Memo to self: "Bob, never eat hot chili before a church service!" While I honestly want to forget it, it is very useful and valuable information that, if remembered, helps to protect myself and the entire congregation from . . . well you can imagine.

During a career in competitive archery that will soon span 60 years, including shooting and coaching, I have tried not to have to learn from the same mistake twice. I work hard to remember all the things I've tried that failed along with all the things I have found that worked. But I am reminded of the Chinese proverb that says, "The weakest ink is mightier that the strongest memory." So, what does that mean to you and me as we go forward teaching and coaching collegiate archers. It means that we should encourage our archers to create and keep an archery journal from the very moment they buy into the addiction, which is tournament archery.

I know. I'm talking to you as an archery coach who is serious about having an impact on his archers' future success and all you're hearing is, "Blah, blah, blah, do more work, blah, blah, blah. I'm sorry, but this is actually where a little bit of guidance from you will have them doing all the work on a project themselves and that will morph into their ability to help themselves to become better and more independent. Ah, now that you look a little more receptive; let's talk about the details.

Why Keep a Journal?

Your students may ask you, "How can a journal help me? And your simple response is, "Help me count the ways!"

- When you show up at practice you must learn to quiet your busy mind and focus on the initial entry while you plan your practice.
- At the end of practice, you will focus once again on what you did in practice, what you learned, what you changed, what went right and/or wrong and what you need to fix, improve, or work on in the next practice.
- You will record any experiments on and changes to your form.
- You will record any changes to your equipment.
- You will record any changes to your setup or tune.
- You will record any scores shot in practice along with any extenuating circumstances or conditions that may have had an effect.
- You will record any scores shot in tournaments along with any noteworthy circumstances or conditions.

Since all these entries are date stamped you will be able to get in your time machine and travel back from the U.S. Indoor Championships you are trying to get ready for to the two previous U.S. Indoor Championships you competed in to review the setups you shot and the results they gave you.

Information like this and comparisons you can make when looking back can often provide your greatest guidance going forward.

What a Deal!

An archery journal costs nothing to start. Your kids can start it in a notebook that they already have or in a free app like Evernote which has a pretty good search function. If they do want to buy something, they can purchase a blank journal anywhere or a generic sport journal in sporting goods stores. If you want the maximum flexibility you can purchase a small three-ring binder and print your own customized pages.

Making A Customized Team Journal

You have a choice now. You can leave them on their own to design their own personalized journal, which is certainly the easiest for you and allows the most motivated of your archers an opportunity to further distance themselves from their teammates and competition, or you can do what I used to do and make a small (5½"x 8½") Team Handbook that includes a Team Roster, Team Schedule, Team Rules, Travel Rules, Shooter/Equipment Data Form, Goals Form, Shot Plotting Scorecards, Tuning Guidelines, and Blank pages for notes. The value of providing useful reference material in the same book that would house your archers journal pages is that it could always be with them and it wouldn't necessarily draw attention to their use of a journal (*see sample page at end*).

Whatever choice you and your kids make concerning your first journal remember that a journal can morph from simple to complex as you get into its use. The next step is for your team to learn how to use a journal to maximize its value.

How to Use an Archery Journal to Your Benefit

Here is what I tell my archers: when you get to practice take a moment to gather your thoughts as you shift your focus from the busy outside world to archery practice.

- Make sure to record today's date and time noting whether this is a practice session or is a competition.
- Note whether you are shooting indoors or outdoors. If indoors, write down what the lighting and temperature are like. When shooting outdoors record how cloudy the day is, along with the temperature, any precipitation and what the wind conditions are.
- Next, state what you plan to work on today. Whether you will be working on form, timing, equipment, tuning, the mental game or just building up your arrow count. Describing your plan in as much detail or as little detail as you think will be beneficial to you later.

    We want to make sure that they record their activity accurately as they want to be able to look back on how much work they are able to accomplish at practice.
- Record minutes of time spent in warm-up at the beginning of the practice and stretching at the end of practice.
- Also, record the number of arrows shot at blank bale, form practice, scoring, to help keep track of arrow count and stamina.
- Make note of any observations in real time while practicing that you may want to refer back to at a later time.
- Make sure to record any changes that they have made to form, equipment, or tuning during today's practice. Note further whether the changes made were temporary or permanent along with related comments and observations.
- Always include notes on what they learned today.
- Maybe the most important thing to write down at the end of every practice is "What I Need to Work on Next." Without that note, by the time your archers write three more papers and take two more tests and come back to practice they're lucky to remember whether they shoot a recurve or a compound much less what they were working on at their most recent practice.

What Else Can We Do?

You can have your archers incorporate their exercise program right into their archery journal to make a more complete record of their efforts but I have another thought that should be even more valuable. I've been thinking about this for a while and I believe you can take your archery journal and your shooting the next level by incorporating three additional forms.

Shooter Data Form This document in intended to record every aspect of your archer's form as it can best be described to serve as a record for future reference. Any time that your archer changes his stance or how he hooks the string, the form should be amended, including the date of the change.

Equipment Data Form This form is used to record every piece of equipment your archer uses including information on backup equipment. In addition, every measurement or detail available on your equipment is recorded so that if something terrible happens you would be able to replace his equipment and set it up to perform with the least amount of difficulty. Naturally, any time that your archer changes any piece of equipment or the way it is set up or tuned you need to amend the form to reflect the change.

Archery Change Log The change log pulls all your archer's records together by providing a single form that you put all changes onto dated in chronological order. Whenever you make a note on your Archery Journal page showing that you made a change to Form, Equipment or Tuning you automatically make a corresponding note on your Change Log and complete the amendment to your Shooter or Equipment Data Form. This will allow your archer to create an historical reference to track changes along with progress and development.

I hope that, after reading this chapter, I have helped you to understand the value and power of an Enhanced Archery Journal. It puts the power of information right in the hands of you and your archers and gives you one more advantage over those who just shoot and hope for the best without taking the time and making the effort to be the best.

JMU Archery Journal

Name _____ **- Date** _____

Practice		Competition		Start Time

Indoor

Lighting		Temperature	
Excellent		Hot	
Adequate		Comfortable	
Poor		Cold	

Outdoor

Weather		Temperature		Precipitation		Wind	
Sunny		Hot		None		Calm	
Partly		Comfortable		Rain		Breeze	
Cloudy		Cold		Snow		Gusty	

What I will work on today?

Form		Timing		Equipment	
Mental Game		Tuning		Arrow Count	

Description:

Activity	Minutes	Arrows	Observations:
Warm-Up			
Blank Bale			
Practice			
Scoring			
Stretching			

What did I learn today?

What did I Change today?

Form		Equipment		Tuning	

What do I need to work on next?

Health & Fitness

Nutrition

Water — Drink min 8 glasses of water daily — Circle One: 1 2 3 4 5 6 7 8 +

Food — Maintain Daily Caloric Intake of _____ — My total calories for today was _____

Exercise

			Today	Tomorrow
Cardio	Perform a minimum of 45 min of aerobic exercise three days a week			
Strength	Perform a minimum of 30 min of weight training three days a week			

170612.10

263

Bob Ryder

About the Author

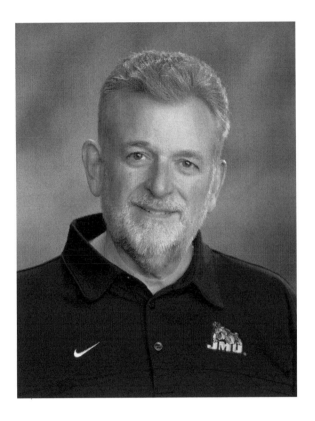

Bob Ryder is 4-time National Collegiate Archery Coach of the Year, a USA Archery Level 4 NTS Coach, a Recipient of the Maurice Thompson Medal of Honor, a past U.S. Intercollegiate All-American and National Champion, past member of the U.S. Archery Team, National Judge, Tournament Director for over 50 National Archery Championships, including National Indoor, Target and Field Championships, past Vice-President and member of the National Archery Association (NAA, now USA Archery) Board of Governors, past Chairman and Executive Committee Member of the College Division of the NAA and member of the James Madison University Athletic Hall of Fame. He served over 20 years as Head Coach of the James Madison University Archery Team which produced 42 All-Americans, 16 National Champions, 23 National Team Titles and 14 World Champions during his tenure.

Bob Ryder

The Watching Arrows Fly Coaching Library

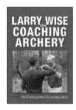

Larry Wise on Coaching Archery
by Larry Wise

The Principles of Coaching Archery, Vol. 1 & 2
by Steve Ruis

Still More on Coaching Archery
by Steve Ruis

Archery Coaching How To's
by Steve Ruis

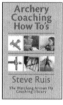

Even More on Coaching Archery
by Steve Ruis

More on Coaching Archery
by Steve Ruis

Coaching Archery
by Steve Ruis

Teaching Archery
by Van Webster

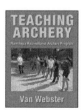

More from Watching Arrows Fly

The Young at Archery
by Hugh D.H. Soar

Professional Archery Technique
by Kirk Ethridge

Why You Suck at Archery
(And What You Can Do About It)
by Steve Ruis

Winning Archery
by Steve Ruis

Confessions of an Archery Mom
by Lorretta Sinclair

Shooting Arrows
(Archery for Adult Beginners)
by Steve Ruis

A Parent's Guide to Archery
by Steve Ruis

Archery for Kids
by Steve Ruis

ProActive Archery
by Tom Dorigatti

267

Bob Ryder

Made in the USA
Middletown, DE
20 December 2021

56352372R10155